Art Treasures of the HERMITAGE

Art Treasures of the

HERMITAGE

text by Pierre Descargues

HARRY N. ABRAMS, INC., PUBLISHERS, NEW YORK

Translated from French by Matila Simon

Standard Book Number: 8109-0023-8
Library of Congress Catalogue Card Number: 72-142741
HARRY N. ABRAMS, INCORPORATED, New York
Printed and bound in Japan

Contents

The HERMITAGE

We do not go to Leningrad as we go to Florence, nor do we visit the Hermitage Museum as we do the Uffizi. To understand the city and its museum, we must remember that Leningrad has scarcely any past. No more than New York, for example, but still enough to confuse the visitor. Under its original name of Saint Petersburg the city rose in 1703, not as a tiny fishing port or a garrison town, but as a capital from the outset. The czar himself had left Moscow and the Kremlin to take up residence there, and for five years he lived in an isba, a log hut that today we would call a construction shack. Thus began a great adventure, comprehensible in no other terms but its own. Let us therefore imagine the government of a distant and powerful country deciding today to indulge itself in a new capital. This capital will obviously be a modern one. Naturally, everybody protests: the site chosen is isolated and unhealthy; the idea is capricious; it will consume resources needed for more urgent matters. The promoter stands firm, calls for building bids, invites foreign architects who, dazzled by the scheme, come willingly. It is not every day that someone proposes to lay out a whole city in one stroke.

Bold new constructions were rising elsewhere at the time: the royal palaces of Stockholm, Copenhagen, and Potsdam, the Place Louis XV in Paris. But on these Russian marshes it is not simply a new quarter that is being built, it is an entire city.

The opposition mounts again. Foreigners cannot know how to build in our tradition, nor for our climate. What will people think of these Italian rhythms in a city so far to the north? Nevertheless, the city rises, and Peter the Great abandons his isba for the palace. He has decided that Russia must emerge from her isolation and from her exalted self-absorption in traditions which have been suffocating her. She must become a modern state like Great Britain, the Netherlands, or France. The country possesses all the necessary natural resources to launch itself on the currents of the world. It needs factories and arsenals; he builds them. At the same time its rulers need palaces that express the latest achievements of architecture, for Peter well understands that authority must move to occupy the new spaces created by new ideas. Since one must have frescoes, he commissions artists to paint them. As for tapestries, he sets up a factory.

Peter the Great set the example and the tone for ensuing generations. The czars and nobility never stopped building. Leningrad is a city of palaces, and one walks there as in an eighteenth-century architectural ideal. This avenue, we think, is Italian. This square is French, but not circumscribed in the usual way. Here, no edict, no adjacent structures have impeded the pleasure of constructing facades of the proper length, of opening streets as wide as the planners wished. Because the city is a direct realization of plans conceived in the freedom of the studio, it lacks those accidents, those unexpected mixtures that add a pleasant quality of human custom to the abstract creations of urbanism. But the colors of the facades—blues, yellows, greens, whites—enliven the conception. And also, in the midst of this careful order, the astonishing churches thrust their gilded onion domes upward, shapes not anticipated in the builders' right-angled symmetries. This powerful surge awakens us—we may be in the northern dream of a Roman or Parisian architect, in a fretwork of canals by a Dutch engineer, but we are also in Russia.

Saint Petersburg provided an immediate and marvelous proving ground for the intellectual values of the eighteenth century, and was for the architecture of the time what Brasilia may be for that of our own period. Yet the new capital remained, as it were, on the country's edge. This is less obvious nowadays, for the passage of time has smoothed away the contrasts and the visitor does not find it unusual that along the Neva there should be these facades topped by sentinel statues and stone vases. But at the time it must have come as a shock—the country had been too long unaware of its own accelerated movement toward the West.

This frozen outlet on the shores of the Baltic suddenly became a magnet attracting everything foreign to Russia. Huge collections of foreign art were established; Rembrandts, Rubenses, Tiepolos, and Poussins imported; Raphael's Vatican loggias re-created. The ideas of the French Encyclopedists were welcomed to a new climate, Voltaire's manuscripts and Diderot's library purchased, and the new collections were arranged according to the latest historical principles. People were attuned to London, Paris, Munich, and Rome. Small wonder that with such interests nobody collected icons or paid attention to native Russian art, suddenly helpless before this influx of new tendencies. Historians tell us that Catherine II replaced one of Rublev's most beautiful iconostases in the Vladimir Cathedral with a Baroque decoration. All the sovereigns, all the princes of the church, did the same in every country of Europe. When a style dies, it must be relinquished.

In Europe, the replacement of a French work by an Italian, of a Dutch work by a French one, simply meant changing one familiar reference for another or substituting one tendency for another. The new shoots were not totally unknown and grew from the same stem. But what was modification in Europe became in Russia a total mutation of species, of inspiration, of language. The choice was obvious: become a convert or perish, and the conversion was to foreign ways. The Hermitage, from its inception, was a foreign museum, as foreign as a museum of Chinese art in London or a museum of European art in Tokyo is today.

Of course, the arts were encouraged in Saint Petersburg, and an academy established for the training of artists. The imperial collections were open to students of the fine arts. Yet, it was not until the nineteenth century that Alexander I decided to create a special gallery in the Hermitage for the Russian school of painting, and there the number of paintings never exceeded seventy-two. It is, moreover, unlikely that such a gallery could have been opened earlier, for the new standards took nearly a century to arouse a strong enough creative movement. In any case, only Westernized Russian artists were admitted; the icon masters were excluded.

This is not surprising. During the same period, Montesquieu spoke of Gothic cathedrals as barbaric. But the schism went even deeper in Russia, cutting off one world from another. There was no contact between what had gone before and what was happening now. The idea itself of separation began to prevail—understandably—for it was necessary to bridge a gap in one day that the Western world had taken 250 years to cross. The Russians had to leap abruptly from the fifteenth to the eighteenth century.

Even today in Leningrad, national and foreign art are separated. The division is far from arbitrary, and corresponds to reality. The two forms of art had been separated and they continue to be. Nevertheless, during the first twenty-five years of the century, Russian and European artists had close relations. Kandinsky, Chagall, Tatlin, Malevich, Pevsner, and Gabo worked toward the same goals as did artists in Paris, Munich, and Milan. Then the understanding ended.

Russia is so constituted that it passes through alternate phases of opening and closing its doors, of drawing toward the outside world and of turning inward on itself. Yet, since the reign of Peter the Great, it has never reconciled its past with its present. Conditions are such that the past has continued to weigh upon all new departures, which necessarily question what went before. Sometimes this rupture is painfully felt, as in a book by Vladimir Solukhin that is entitled *Lettres du Musée Russe*. The author goes to Leningrad and discovers that nobody thinks very much of the Russian National Museum in the Mikhailovsky Palace, which contains national painting from the oldest icons to the works of contemporary artists. He no doubt exaggerates in stating that the Muscovite artist Andrei Rublev, the greatest painter of the fifteenth century, is still unrecognized, but what lingers from the book is the author's desperate cry: "We thought we possessed nothing. Our traditions were broken." I have no doubt that the same distress was felt by Russian masons working for Peter the Great, as it was felt by Russian artists when the German-born Catherine II filled her Hermitage with the hundreds of paintings that her ambassadors purchased at public auctions in Paris and Amsterdam. "We thought we possessed nothing." If we still hear that cry at a time when the USSR has become one of the most powerful nations in the world, it may be because the old national character, enshrouded in the smoke of ecclesiastical incense, in folk music, in icons that preserved the Byzantine aesthetic, has always been rejected by the innovators but is nevertheless by no means dead. This is one of the constants of the country. For Russia to advance she must cut loose from her past, but at the same time she cannot forget it.

These ruptures, deep as saber cuts, had at least one advantage understood by all pioneers. Nothing is allowed to impede their progress. The new land that they cultivate is infinite, and they will lucidly carry their project further than anybody else. This was true of Peter the Great, of Catherine II; it was true of the nobility; it was true of the bourgeois who began to collect art at the beginning of the twentieth century. They were more zealous than other connoisseurs. This was also true of the curators who classified and arranged the prodigious abundance of works turned over to them after the Revolution. Perhaps it was because they were all so far removed from other men and other ideas that they were more objective and more comprehensive.

All during the building of the city and the accompanying formation of its art collections, a certain atmosphere of daring and keen judgment remained in force. This atmosphere has endured for two centuries.

THE GROWTH OF THE COLLECTIONS

The name Hermitage, which evokes retreat and solitude, was given more from force of habit than from mockery to the group of overlapping palaces called individually the Great Hermitage, the Little Hermitage, the New Hermitage, and the Winter Palace. Seen from the outside, the buildings harmonize a century and a half of different architectural trends. The ensemble is one of those gigantic constructions like Versailles, the Louvre, the royal palaces of Vienna and Munich, the Escorial. They are all oversized, supposedly useless and yet constantly used, for nations need these unlivable enormities in which they discover that it is as right to build out of all proportion for man's ideals and his dreams as it is to erect great cathedrals for God. But there is an important difference —a palace revolves around the thousand and one moments in the day of one man only, the prince: his sleep and his councils, his banquets and balls, his lovemaking and his theater, his reading, his music, his celebrations and his solitude, and each activity necessitates suites of different rooms. Only one vault is required for the celebration of the Mass.

Until now, the Hermitage has been spared the radical decisions of modern museography: the history of painting unfolds on the walls of rooms built as the setting for an emperor's day. However,

Hans Holbein the Elder (German; c. 1460–c. 1524).
Portrait of Holbein's Sons

since some of the rooms were conceived for the exhibition of paintings in an epoch when nobody dreamed that a painting might ever be shown outside a palace, there is a unity of splendor within the museum's diversity. This does not always make for comfortable viewing; indeed, the paintings are hung almost frame to frame. From the windows, the brightness of the snow-covered frozen Neva is reflected in the glass that protects some of the paintings. But this crowding makes it possible to see about two thousand paintings and to discover that it is not always bad to twist one's neck to contemplate a particular work. One might even say that the difficulty stimulates attention.

Figures do not always give a clear idea of size (it is, for example, difficult to understand what 250,000 square feet of exhibition halls represent); so perhaps we may realize the extent of the Hermitage by noting that in the four palaces one can look out of 1,945 windows, walk up and down 117 staircases, and open 1,786 doors. Piranesi could not have done better. The large halls are not all utilized and the public is limited to a mere 300 rooms. Slightly more than 2,000 of the museum's 8,000 paintings are on view. The print collection comprises 500,000 engravings. There are more than 40,000 entries in the catalogue of drawings.

The Hermitage is not only a museum of Western art, but in addition contains Indian, Chinese, ancient Egyptian, Mesopotamian, Persian (the Sassanian collection is famous), pre-Columbian, Grecian, Roman, Prehistoric, Scythian, and Urartian art. The museum also has collections of textiles, armor, tapestries, faience, porcelain, coins, engraved gems, ivories, furniture, and jewelry. There is even a section devoted to the history of the Russian people. It is one of the few general museums of the world and if it is possible to establish degrees of wealth, the Hermitage would rank second in diversity after the Louvre. Many studies are possible in Leningrad. The library contains remarkable illuminated French manuscripts. The Ethnology Museum displays the art of the American Indian (Alaska was Russian before it became part of the United States) and African art. Such variety is a credit to the city which has continued to be not only a port open on the world, but also a center of culture, capable of housing the Taurine Venus, the Pergamum reliefs, and the gold or felt artifacts of the Altai civilizations of Central Asia.

14

Albrecht Dürer
(German; 1471–1528).
Virgin and Child

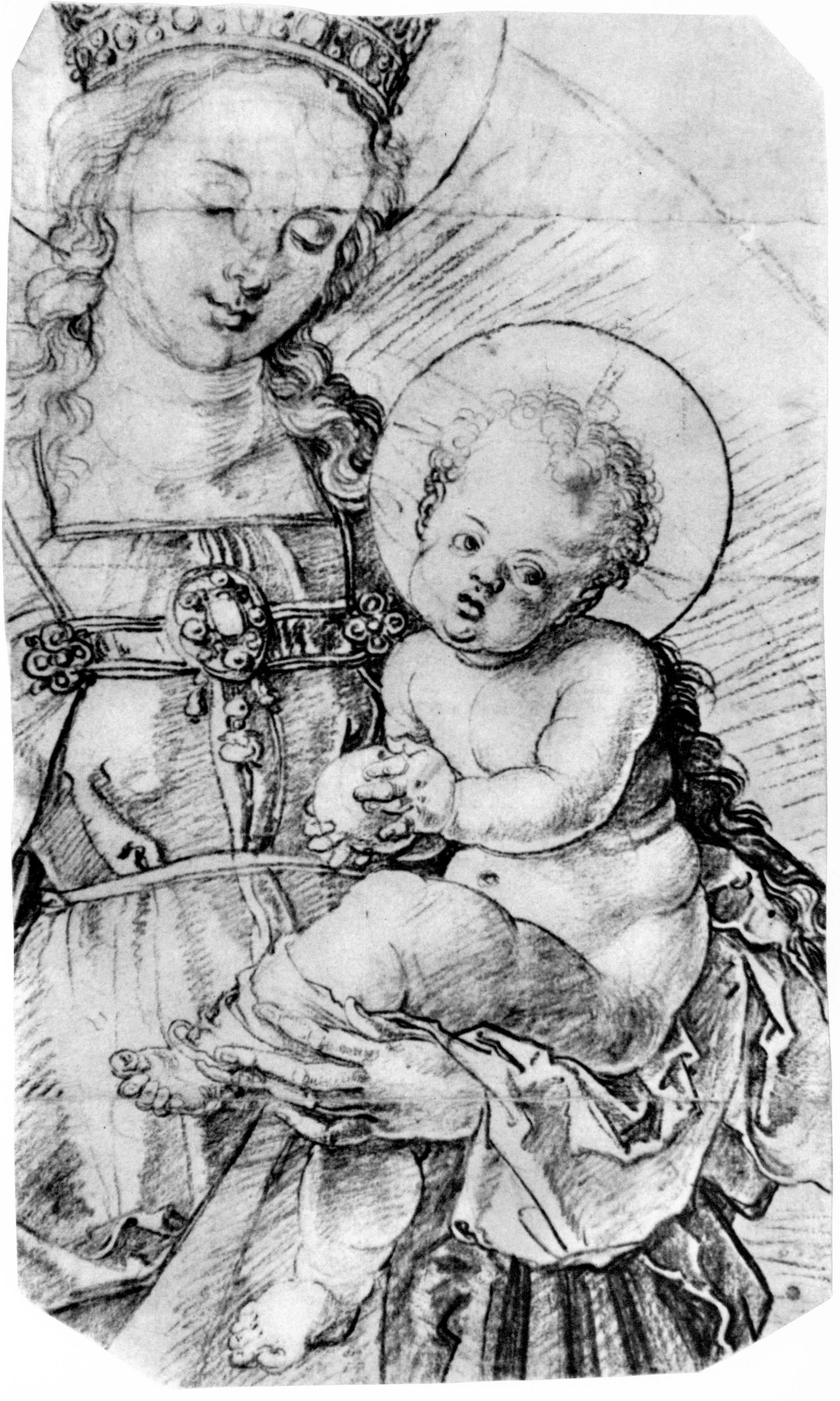

Intellectual curiosity must have been very lively in Saint Petersburg; otherwise the new palaces along the Neva could never have accumulated as much wealth in two centuries as Paris amassed in twice that length of time.

Entrance into the museum is so arranged that it seems to be devoted primarily to Russian history. Peter the Great sits in a glass case, his impressive figure wearing his customary dress, his face duplicated in wax by his court sculptor, Rastrelli. Objects from the epoch preceding his ascent to the throne are there merely to indicate continuity—it is Peter who dominates. His throne has been preserved, and throngs of Russians walk on floors made of rare woods and go into the throne room where the imperial eagle has been replaced by a map of the Soviet Republics. The guide informs the astonished visitors that the map (ninety square feet) is made of forty-five thousand precious and semiprecious stones. Next is a room constructed of malachite. Then, swimming in glory and luxury, one comes to a room hung with 330 portraits of the generals who defeated Napoleon. The Hermitage is Russian in its eulogy of its sovereigns and soldiers, Russian in its history, and foreign in its works of art. It is a little as though an immense museum of Indian art were installed in a national history museum in London. People visit the Hermitage to rub elbows with the luxury and abundance of a vanished world; they go with no idea of recrimination, out of the need for the elementary splendor of gold and gems.

This splendor is perhaps the most unpleasing path. Nevertheless, it is the most frequented and doubtless the best one by which to reach that other luxury in which, with the least costly materials —canvas, wood, paint, stone, earth, or paper—man's works reach heights unknown in gold or jewels. What strikes us at the Hermitage is that the same respect is paid to rubies and malachite as to Titian and Matisse. Elsewhere, these two forms of wealth tend more and more to part company. Here they remain together.

The history of these eight thousand paintings does not begin with a visit by the czar to an artist's studio and the purchase of some paintings. It does not start with one of those personal anecdotes such as we have about Francis I and Leonardo da Vinci or Pope Julius II and Michelangelo. It begins with a half-century delay in the purchase of living art. True, the first purchase is a masterpiece, *David's Farewell to Jonathan* by Rembrandt, acquired forty-seven years after the artist's death. The story would perhaps have been better if the collections had begun with the acquisition of a painting by Oudry or Nattier, two artists whom the czar had vainly invited to his new city to share in his great project. But the rule is that one may stand in awe of the dead before liking the living, and so the imperial collections began with a Rembrandt.

And that is perhaps significant. In fact, if we make a rapid survey of the paintings in the Hermitage, we note at once the massive predominance of Flemish and Dutch works, principally of the seventeenth century. Then comes the French section with as many late nineteenth- and early twentieth-century paintings as from the period between the fifteenth and eighteenth centuries. A fine group of Italian paintings dates from the thirteenth to the eighteenth century. German paintings, one-third the number of the Italian, trail far behind. Following them in descending order of quantity are English and Austrian works, and finally Swedish, Danish, Norwegian, Finnish, Hungarian, and Czechoslovakian.

We notice immediately the small place granted in these Russian collections to works by artists of neighboring countries. This indicates a choice made above the level of local trade; despite the close

TITIAN (Italian; 1477/87–1576)

Danaë

Painted about 1553–54

Oil on canvas, 46 1/2 × 73 5/8″

Catalogue No. 121.* *Formerly Crozat Collection*

In his notes to the albums of engravings of works in the Crozat Collection, J.-P. Mariette pronounced this painting the most precious in the collection. There are variants of this *Danaë* in the Prado (one of the *poesias* offered by Titian to Philip II), in the Vienna Museum, and in the Naples Museum. This last, once owned by Cardinal Farnese, is the one that was viewed in Titian's studio by Michelangelo and Vasari, and about which Michelangelo remarked, "If this man [Titian] had as much knowledge of art and drawing as he has natural talent in copying from life, he would be unsurpassable, for he has great understanding and a lively, brilliant style."

Michelangelo's opinion of Titian's lack of artistic education was widespread at the time and not simply the incomprehension of one artist of another's work. Vasari also mentions a statement by Sebastiano del Piombo: "If Titian had only gone to Rome and seen the ancient statues and the works of Michelangelo and Raphael, and if he had also studied drawing, he would have produced astonishing things." This remark sounds like some eighteenth-century critic's lament over Rembrandt: "Oh, if only he had been born in Rome!" Such was the pressure that the academicians were to exert throughout the

centuries and which was to last until the Impressionists. This does not mean that academicism was sterile. The simple division between the draftsman and colorist leads to the absurdity of an aesthetic war, no doubt because in art each is engaged wholeheartedly and cannot progress except by opposing the other.

The fantasy of the Danaë theme seems to have been primarily attractive to colorists. If we compare Titian's versions with those of Tiepolo (Stockholm) and Rembrandt (Hermitage), we see that for Titian the myth was only incidental, while for Rembrandt it became a source of mystery and scattered erotic allusions, and for Tiepolo a fine occasion for theatrical effects. The Venetian simply enjoyed painting a beautiful nude and contrasting her flesh with the tawny skin of the servant. The *Danaë* is one of countless nudes who became, according to the setting, Antiope, Venus, Eve, a nymph, Religion, Diana, Europa, a bacchante, or Flora, and was, in reality, the celebration of great sensual pleasure.

* Catalogue numbers are taken from the two-volume Hermitage catalogue edited by P. F. Levinson-Lessing (Leningrad, 1958).

Francesco Francia (Italian; 1450/53–1517).
An Ancient Sacrifice

Ercole de' Roberti
(Italian; c. 1451/56–1496).
Members of the Este Family

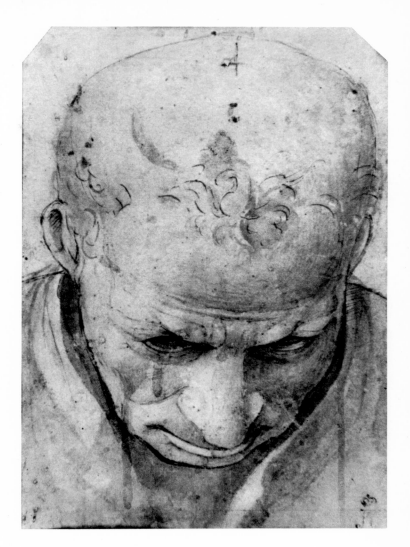

Luca Signorelli (Italian; 1445/50–1523).
Head of an Old Man

Piero di Cosimo (Italian; 1462–1521).
Head of an Old Man

political and commercial ties between the Russians and Germans, Russian collectors from the start joined European connoisseurs in the desire for seventeenth-century Flemish and Dutch paintings. The "Golden Century" had, in fact, just begun to gain an international reputation and to move out of national into foreign collections, with works suddenly available as a whole generation of collectors died off. Despite this new interest, Italian painting retained its position of supremacy. Canaletto and Amigoni were called to London, Pellegrini to Düsseldorf and Paris, Tiepolo to Würzburg and Madrid, Bellotto to Vienna, Dresden, and Warsaw. A great number of Italian architects went to Saint Petersburg, where their work may still be admired. Italian painters were less fortunate, for the works with which they decorated the palaces have not survived the passage of time, many having been destroyed in fires. We therefore know little about their contribution. It is possibly absurd that we feel the impression of a Dutch stamp on the early collection, but the feeling persists. In addition, the Russians did not attract the most famous living Italians, and fifteenth- and sixteenth-century works signed by the most glorious names could no longer be found. Collectors had hunted them for years and a great many had found their way into royal collections that were, if not definitive, stable enough for the moment. We must finally take into account certain similarities between the Russians and the Dutch: they had, for example, a common distrust of the nude figures which Italians found so easy and natural. It is also easy to imagine how Rembrandt's *David's Farewell to Jonathan*, poignantly embracing and dressed in Oriental garb, might constitute not only a point of departure for the collections, but also the symbol of a profound choice and a lasting trend.

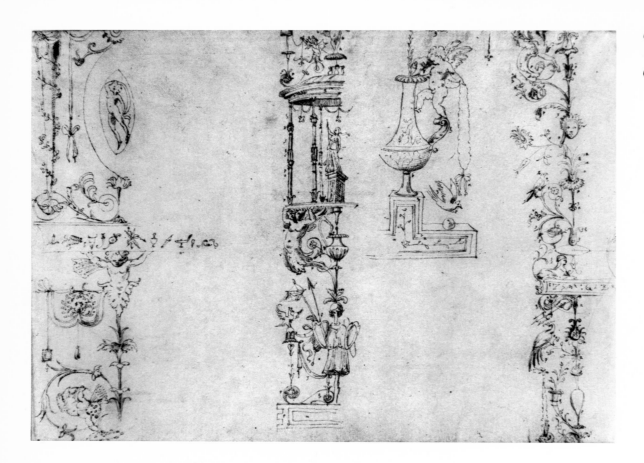

Giovanni da Udine
(Italian; c. 1487–1564).
Grotesques from the Vatican Loggias

Tintoretto (Italian; 1518/19–1584).
Studies of Male Nudes

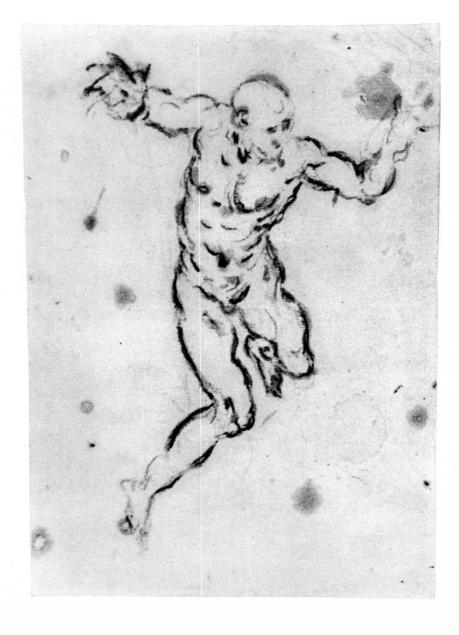

Luca Cambiaso (Italian; 1527–1585).
Adoration of the Magi

Giovanni Battista Tiepolo (Italian; 1696–1770).
Study of Figures (subject unknown)

It is hard to imagine a sovereign without some interest in art. Some European rulers had perhaps been surprised by Louis XIV's actual employment of the writers, artists, musicians, and men of the theater whom he attached to his court. But the success of this royal propaganda had only strengthened the need of all of them to be surrounded by artists and works of art, if for no other reason than to rival the French king. For a long time, the sovereigns had had agents at the great sales of paintings in Paris, Vienna, and Amsterdam, as well as emissaries close to the heirs of great collectors. The Russians arrived on the scene a bit late. At the beginning of the eighteenth century, the Elector of Saxony, then king of Poland, owned works by Rubens, Giorgione, Rembrandt, and Poussin, and was seen to purchase the entire painting collection of the Duke of Modena. Even before he became emperor, the young Frederick of Prussia bought Watteaus and Lancrets. The great rulers competed for paintings, each trying to do the other out of a masterpiece. Extravagance was obviously mixed with the pleasure of a good bargain. Frederick the Great boasted of having obtained fourteen French paintings of incomparable quality "for a song," and on another occasion declared that eight paintings he had just purchased gave him more pleasure than "the king of Poland had from his whole Modena gallery." The Russian entry into this already active market obviously made people sit up and take notice.

The collectors immediately realized that they were now faced with powerful rivals. The agents, licensed or speculative, determined not to neglect such wealthy clients. Russian envoys were soon visibly seeking antiquities in Rome and searching for paintings in Brussels, Antwerp, and London. It is not surprising that their first purchases were considered cultural obligations. The first museums built in Saint Petersburg date from 1709: they were a naval museum housing models of vessels built in Russian shipyards and a *Kunstkamera*, a kind of natural history museum that included a library, an astronomical observatory, collections of minerals, stuffed animals, and a number of natural curiosities. A visit to the Archduke Ferdinand's science collection in the Amras castle in Austria today gives us an idea of what the Kunstkamera was like. The collections of Albert of Bavaria and of the Emperor Rudolph II began with similar accumulations of current knowledge.

The collections of Peter the Great, however, must be considered as something secondary, one element among all the others he attempted in Saint Petersburg. More than objects, he wanted men— as directors of artistic projects, professors, or court portraitists. This trend continued after Peter's successors. Many artists went to Saint Petersburg: the painter Caravaque of Marseilles, the Italian sculptor Rastrelli, the Italian portraitist Rotari, the Venetian Fontebasso, who worked in the city for two years (1761–62), the French portraitist Louis Tocqué, who also stayed for two years, and the Dane Virgilius Erichsen, who remained in Russia from 1757 to 1762. The English artist Richard Brompton died in the new capital; the Austrian Johann Baptist Lampi later lived there for five years. Several French artists forged their careers in Russia: Louis-Joseph Maurice, Louis-Joseph Lorrain, Jean-François Lagrenée, Gabriel Doyen, Jean-Baptiste Le Prince, and Jean Voille. The most famous artists were not among those who stayed the longest, nor did the desired master always accept the royal invitation. Peter the Great wanted Oudry; he got Caravaque instead. Elizabeth wanted Nattier and obtained Tocqué. Similarly, Frederick the Great sought Boucher and Carle van Loo and had to be content with Blaise-Nicolas Lesueur, Charles-Amédée van Loo, and principally Antoine Pesne. Stanislas Augustus of Poland likewise had J. B. Pillement, André Le Brun, Bacciarelli,

Peter Paul Rubens
(Flemish; 1577–1640).
The Three Graces (after Raphael)

Peter Paul Rubens
The Head of Cyrus Brought to Queen Tomyris

PETER PAUL RUBENS (Flemish; 1577–1640)
Union of Earth and Water

Painted about 1615–20

Oil on canvas, 87 1/2 × 71"

Catalogue No. 464

The Hermitage owns forty-two works by Rubens. The collection includes a work from the first years of his return to Antwerp (a sketch for the *Adoration of the Magi* painted for Saint Paul's Church), sketches for the Medici Gallery of the Louvre (especially interesting to Parisian tourists), portraits, allegories, landscapes, and religious and historical subjects. Sketches or finished works, the ensemble is large and varied enough to give a rounded idea of the artist's genius.

This allegory, in which Rubens painted only the figures, is the kind of picture in which the meaning matters little but which holds our attention by its beauty. The subject is a marriage between a marine figure, whose muscular body belies the age suggested by his beard, and a young woman. The man carries a trident and is followed by a Triton blowing on a conch. Fame crowns the girl while a pet tiger roars. Cupids play in the water. For us, all that matters is that the work is by Rubens.

When we come upon a Rubens among the works of other masters in a museum, it impresses us from the first as being the most open and forthright, with no secret meanings, and no double or ambiguous images hidden in the shadows. Painting, for Rubens, was an exercise in pictorial skill, which he was able to apply to any subject. But, although his ability certainly equaled that of the most powerful Italian artists, Rubens is more in contact with the forces of the earth and flesh. By comparison, the Italians seem more intellectual and abstract. There is in Rubens something of the reality of the Great God Pan which Christianity repressed, although this did not keep him from being one of the most eminent painters of the Crucifixion. One imagines that his search for the powerful voice he heard went far beyond a simple curiosity and interest in antiquity.

Peter Paul Rubens
The Head of Seneca and other studies
for the *Miracles of St. Ignatius Loyola*

Peter Paul Rubens
Portrait of Helena Fourment

Peter Paul Rubens
Portrait of Rubens's Son

Bellotto, and Norblin de la Gourdaine. The current flowed in both directions, with Western artists moving eastward to join their patrons, and Russian students going to Paris to study with such men as Greuze and Pigalle. An immense time lag was considerably overcome, not only in the arts but also in the art of collecting. Here we might recall that a "Collection of Prints after Famous Paintings of the Dresden Royal Gallery" was published in Saxony as early as 1753, at a time when the Russian imperial collections were not very important or valuable. Thus, it should be noted that Russia moved ahead of Dresden by the creation of a teaching academy.

We were speaking of Rembrandt. For half a century, the czars continued to purchase Dutch art and Catherine II's acquisitions never wholly departed from this tendency. However, the coming of French painters to Russia, the presence of Falconet, who worked on the equestrian statue of Peter the Great, the increasingly frequent trips to Paris by noblemen who had themselves painted by Frenchmen, the correspondence between first Elizabeth's favorites, and then Catherine II herself and the Encyclopedists made French art as welcome in Russia as it was in the capitals of Central Europe beginning with Potsdam. In addition, all of Europe spoke French and this could only facilitate the diffusion of French painting. The shiploads of paintings that arrived in Saint Petersburg included works by Watteau as well as Poussin, and both artists were upheld by the praises of Parisian writers and artists. This did not stem the avalanche of works by Mieris, Dou, Wouwermans, Ruisdael, Van Ostade, and others.

Very soon, however, another method of enrichment was to be added to the purchase of paintings at auctions, that of dealing directly with collectors in order to buy up entire collections. This expeditious process had the advantage of eliminating connoisseurs without huge sums at their disposal and left the field to the ruling princes. Louis XIV and Augustus of Saxony had resorted to this practice earlier. It was a fine coup for Catherine II when she thus acquired the collection of Count von Brühl, minister of that same Augustus, who had been closely connected with the formation of the Saxon collections and had had the idea for what must be called the first rooms especially lit for the exhibition of paintings. The Brühl purchase, in 1769, brought some Rubenses and the small copies of Bellotto's Dresden works. Three years later, four hundred paintings from the collection of the Parisian financier Crozat added new Dutch and French works, more Rubenses, and a group of Italians: Raphael, Giorgione, Titian, Veronese, Carracci, Guercino, and Tibaldi. The next collection of 198 paintings had belonged to Robert Walpole, and came from England in 1778. This acquisition added to the already rich group of Rubenses and increased the number of Rembrandts; it also introduced into Russia a French painter unknown in France, Poussin's brother-in-law, Gaspard Dughet, whose works had been seen hitherto only in Rome and in London. In 1784, 119 paintings from the collection of Count de Baudouin further strengthened the Dutch section. By these swift strokes, large groups of masterpieces enriched the imperial collections without modifying their original orientation. Even today, the Hermitage retains the formidable advantage it gained by these eighteenth-century harvests of Dutch and Flemish painting.

Although the French Revolution destroyed the bridges that reached from the banks of the Seine to those of the Neva, the ties were reestablished early in the nineteenth century by the return of Voille to Russia, by the exiled Vigée-Lebrun, and J. L. M. Mosnier, who taught in Saint Petersburg until his death. But the exchanges suffered from the effects of the Russian and Crimean campaigns, so that Romanticism and Neoclassicism are almost unrepresented in the imperial collections. In addition, despite the exceptional presence of six works by Caspar David Friedrich, very few exam-

Anthony van Dyck (Flemish; 1599–1641).
Pentecost

Anthony van Dyck
Studies for the Holy Family

ples of German Romanticism are included. Aristocratic connoisseurs would respond later on to Delaroche, Horace Vernet, Meissonier, the Barbizon artists (Diaz, Rousseau, etc.), but it was the English artists Christine Robertson and George Dawe, the German Franz Krüger, and finally Winterhalter who painted portraits of the czars and nobles. Winterhalter did not even have to go to Russia—his models posed for him in Wiesbaden, Baden, Paris, or Geneva.

One might say that in the nineteenth century Germany played a role comparable to that of France a century before. Germany brought a feeling for analysis and a sense of staging: the first may be seen in the classification of collections; the second in a cult of the antique, which perhaps did more harm to Russian artists than to those of any other country. In Saint Petersburg, as elsewhere in Europe, people were dedicated to the restoration of an ideal that was really more Roman than Athenian, as may be seen in the curious "antique painting gallery," a highly interesting monstrosity, and a pure and simple invention by Hiltensperger according to his notion of an ancient fresco. The conception is, of course, much more nineteenth-century than Greek or Roman, but cannot be condemned for that. It is a document on the glorification of the antique. Upon the advice of Reiffenstein, a friend of Winckelmann, Catherine II had indulged herself by having Raphael's Vatican loggias copied by the painter Unterberger and the architect Quarenghi. This copy has become very valuable with the passage of time, since it preserves the condition of the original of two centuries ago. Everything here was contrived, but the dream of Greece amid the ice and snow is one of the conspicuous characteristics of the century.

Besides, the purchasing policy was modified, for the quantity of works acquired began to influence the choice of what was needed. Russian agents set out to find rare works, bearing in mind the treasures already obtained and hoping to round out the collections. The curators wanted to make the Hermitage a coherent ensemble representing the different schools of painting. Taste had also improved. In 1815, an important group of Spanish paintings was added to the collections previously limited in this area to sentimental Murillos and the fashionable figures of Mengs. The acquisition corresponds historically to the discovery of Spain by writers of Romantic literature and to the political crisis that forced the nobility and the Spanish church to dispose of their property. A second discovery visible in the Hermitage collections was that of the Primitives. By a strange coincidence, Prosper Mérimée, defender of the cathedrals, became interested in Russian history and began his

Pieter van Laer (Dutch; 1592?–1642).
Landscape with a Bridge

REMBRANDT (Dutch; 1606–1669)

Sacrifice of Abraham

Painted in 1635

Oil on canvas, 76 × 52 3/8"

Catalogue No. 727.   Formerly Walpole Collection

This *Sacrifice of Abraham* is one of the most striking examples of Rembrandt's Baroque period, which corresponds to the first years of his life in Amsterdam. Even before he reached the age of thirty, the painter gathered around him the liveliest young talent in the Netherlands—Backer, Bol, Van den Eeckhout, Flinck, and others. These were his true disciples, the men who remained faithful to the ideas that had first attracted them to the young master. In his studio a new movement was born, which resumed in an original manner the direction first indicated by the Utrecht painters and by Pieter Lastmann, Rembrandt's teacher, and which tried to offer the Netherlands an art noble by the standards of the time, that is, Biblical, mythological, and allegorical. Most portraitists, landscapists, genre and still-life painters opposed this tendency and Rembrandt's studio remained its only source. This noble tendency provided great decorative pieces for the Stathouder's residence and the Amsterdam Town Hall, but the wealthy connoisseurs who flocked around Rubens in Antwerp had no counterparts in the Netherlands—"great" painting lost its battle to the other types of work. The quality of this *Sacrifice of Abraham,* as well as the *Blinding of Samson* (Frankfurt), the *Night Watch* (Amsterdam), and the *Conspiracy of Julius Civilis* (Stockholm), make us wonder what the painter's career might have been if he had been offered such walls to paint on as were given to all painters in Italy.

The theme of Abraham prevented from accomplishing his murderous act by the intervention of an angel is not very often treated in painting. It requires a dramatic temperament. One of the most striking paintings on the subject is by Caravaggio (Uffizi), who emphasizes the fear of the young man whose head is held down against the ground. Venice has two eighteenth-century versions of the theme by Vincenzo Damini and by Bencovich. In both of these, the old man holds up his victim and prepares to stab him while preventing him from falling. No one but Rembrandt seems to have had the idea of obliterating the face of the victim beneath the executioner's hand, a highly expressive idea that contrasts dramatically with the brightness of the beautiful body extended as though trustfully. The British Museum has a drawing showing an early stage of the composition. The idea of the hand hiding the face is already present, and there is another suggestion that Rembrandt later abandoned in the painting—the victim seems to strain toward this power that he has accepted, fatal as it may be.

In this painting, Rembrandt achieved a powerful and definitive formula that shows heaven and earth on equal terms. Between the two domains, the astonishing dagger remains suspended in its fall.

Rembrandt (Dutch; 1606–1669). *A Clump of Trees with Farmhouses Along a Road*

biography of Peter the Great at the same time that the curator of the Hermitage visited The Hague to purchase works by Van Eyck, Gossaert, Provost, and Van der Weyden.

That was in 1850. One would expect that this evolution in taste indicated a true widening of perspective. It was actually accompanied by a contraction, as if it were impossible to like something new without simultaneously discarding something old, or as if the human span of interest remained constant. We should not be surprised. Total open-mindedness, the acceptance of all tendencies, is equivalent to indifference. What is removed from one side of the scale must also be taken from the other. Indiscriminate, greedy, disorganized acquisition corresponding to a mad passion for art is followed by an appreciation that assumes something of the scientific and believes itself to be objective. Such objectivity is obviously relative and deceptive. In art, a gluttony that makes no effort at justification may be preferable to that erudite sense of diversion that analyzes all its motives and arranges them in neat categories. So ends the love of art, which no theory can justify. Connoisseurs flourish in a measured and balanced world, where there is no north without a south, no east without a west, but such an atmosphere is not entirely favorable to love. We may, however, have confidence in human beings; they are capable of love under any circumstances, and the order imposed by history is far from being the worst condition. The objectivity to which it aspires may even be understood as the conclusion of the intimate rapport between the collector and the work of art, as the entrance of the work onto neutral terrain where anyone may take it as he pleases.

The transition begins with the concept of a real museum, a building intended for the exhibition of paintings and the presentation of sculpture and art objects. The Russian museum was set up in

Rembrandt
The Parable of the Laborers in the Vineyards

Rembrandt
Polish Officer

Rembrandt
Woody Landscape with a Horseman

Philips Koninck (Dutch; 1619–1688). *Landscape with Farmhouses*

Jacob van Ruisdael (Dutch; 1628/29–1682). *View of Amsterdam*

the German manner. This is explained, on the one hand, by the rift between France and Russia due to the Napoleonic wars and, on the other, by the growth of various German historical schools which in the nineteenth century began to supersede the French. Two Frenchmen, Thoré-Burger, the discoverer of Vermeer, and Paul Lacroix, called the Bibliophile Jacob, worked on identification, but Russian researchers frequently sought the advice of the director of the Berlin museum, G. F. Waagen, a man of great erudition who had done much to develop Prussian collections and who corrected many Russian attributions. It is also significant that, for the plan of their museum, the Russians turned to Leo von Klenze, the Munich architect who had proved his ability by constructing the Glyptothek and Pinakothek, buildings that combine the characteristics of palace and fortress. In these colossal museums, paintings are hung almost from floor to ceiling, in a display that aims primarily at symmetry. This kind of arrangement is not very different from that adopted by Catherine II in her palace at Tsarkoye-Selo, where paintings are separated only by simple gilt moldings to compose a continuous wall. However, such sobriety was not enough—sculptured columns, stucco ceilings, and intricate door frames added the required touches of luxury, while antique chairs, vases, and gigantic lighting fixtures enhanced the impression of wealth. Art was to be glorified like royalty, an association of splendors that seems irredeemably linked.

In Saint Petersburg it is rather painful to pass from Rastrelli's light, almost playful facades to the heavy, austere Roman frontals of Von Klenze. Indeed, the entrance to the museum at first sight seems an aberration. Ten atlantes, tons of granite sculptured by Terebenev, display their huge forms to support a light terrace. This is, however, a hint of the interior, where artistic considerations will prevail over architectural ones. Going from room to room, we discover a festival of different architectural styles. We pass from the Classical to the Oriental, from a vaulted ceiling to one supported by columns, from marquetry flooring to marble tiles. It is an education in the history of architecture and interior decoration.

When the museum was officially opened on February 5, 1852, the ground floor displayed Classical sculpture, bronzes, painted vases, and Siberian antiquities—the gold objects of the Altai civilizations first collected by Peter the Great. Paintings were exhibited on the next floor. It was obvious that the time had passed when works were hung according to recognized affinities without paying attention to the nationality of the artist. Everything was arranged by schools, the collections being divided into seven sections: Italian, Spanish, French, Flemish, Dutch, English, and Russian. For Russian art had finally been admitted to the Hermitage, although it was not to remain for long. While the museum still contains the artifacts of those regions of Central Asia which are now Soviet Republics, it has parted company with its Russian artists. They are installed, more conveniently it is true, in the National Museum in the Mikhailovsky Palace.

The opening of one of the most modern museums in Europe put Saint Petersburg on a cultural footing that enabled it to compete with other capitals. A sweeping rearrangement of the imperial collections lay behind this glorious display. The Russians had made a survey of the paintings scattered about in the different royal palaces, the Winter Palace as well as those in the environs—Peterhof, Pavlovsk, Gatchina, Tsarkoye-Selo, Oranienbaum. This was doubtless necessary, although it would seem that the quantity discovered led to dismay rather than general rejoicing. In all, 4,552 paintings were counted, examined, and classified. It was decided to put 815 in the museum, while 804 others went out to decorate the various imperial residences again, and 1,369 were put in storage. The rest were declared uninteresting and suitable for disposal. Most of these (1,219 to be exact) were offered for sale in 1854.

Such a sale is not unique in the history of museums. The Guggenheim Museum in New York has recently sold dozens of paintings by Kandinsky. But it is rather strange that the commission set up to separate the wheat from the chaff should have placed in the sale category paintings by such famous artists as Lucas van Leyden, Pieter Lastmann, Chardin, and Natoire, works which fortunately were sold to Russian collectors and came back to the Hermitage after the 1917 Revolution. But anyone who has ever participated in the work of an art jury knows that thousands of entries must be accepted or rejected within a few days; decisions must be made quickly and are therefore sometimes mistaken. The choices made here were not apparently dictated by any systematic aesthetic denial; nobody rejects Chardin and Lucas van Leyden at the same time.

The important thing was that Saint Petersburg had a museum. This overcame a time lag when we remember that Basel had one in 1661, Oxford in 1683, London in 1754, Kassel in 1760, Florence in 1737, the Vatican in 1772, Stockholm in 1792, and that one of Napoleon's first concerns was the opening of museums in Venice, Milan, and Amsterdam. The Saint Petersburg museum belonged to what might be called the second generation of nineteenth-century museums, the generation that laid the groundwork for museography and brought about the construction, in Berlin (1828) as well as Munich (1830–36), of enormous temples where the cult of art was celebrated with all the necessary solemnity.

In reality, the Hermitage was not open to the general public, for this was an imperial museum that belonged first to the czar. Court etiquette was required for entrance, and visitors wore evening dress and announced their names.

This formality was perhaps the reason that the Hermitage, although it really belonged more and more to its curators and its visitors and less and less to its owners, did not attract the great flow of gifts generally offered to a national collection. This was also undoubtedly due to the habit of Russian collectors of setting up their own museums. There were certain palaces that one could visit in both Saint Petersburg and Moscow, and perhaps the nobles thought that they could thus rival the czar. We must not overlook, however, two lavish gifts, one of English paintings in 1910, and one of Italian works in 1912, although both were small in comparison to what a museum like the Louvre receives constantly.

Once the Hermitage had been filled, it revealed the unevenness of its riches, and the curators set to fill the gaps. Their first concern was to build up the Italian collection, a task they accomplished with considerable skill, for they were not the only ones in the field. The Germans, English, French, and Austrians were solidly entrenched in Italy, and yet the Russians brought off some difficult transactions. By the nineteenth century, only a very few of the approximately thirty paintings definitely attributed to Leonardo da Vinci were still available, all the others being in national institutions whose statutes forbade resale. Two were acquired by the Louvre—the *Portrait of Isabella d'Este* and the *Annunciation*. Munich bought the *Madonna with the Carnation*, and the Hermitage bought two others—the *Madonna Litta*, so called for its previous owner, the Milanese Duke Litta, and the *Benois Madonna* that turned up as a surprise in the exhibition of treasures from Russian private collections held in Saint Petersburg in 1909. Italian strolling musicians had brought it into Russia at some forgotten time. It had belonged to Prince Kurakhin in Astrakhan, who eventually

ANTOINE WATTEAU (French; 1684–1721)
La Boudeuse

Painted about 1718

Oil on canvas, 16 1/2 × 13 1/2"

Catalogue No. 4120.   Formerly Stroganov Collection

Even the most favorable of Watteau's contemporaries were always somewhat guarded in their remarks about his works. Caylus wrote that "his compositions have no purpose; they do not express the contest of any passions, and consequently lack one of the most piquant aspects of painting." And Mariette observed: "Each figure that issues from the hand of this excellent man has such real and natural character that it captures all our attention by itself and has no need for the composition of a great theme." Which is only to turn Caylus's reservations into admiration.

Nothing happens in a Watteau painting, or rather nothing comes to a head. The figures make signs to each other, but do not meet. That the *Embarkation for Cythera* has become, following the latest critical studies, a *Return from Cythera* changes nothing, for the lonely figures moving forward have been only momentarily united. Watteau does not provide apotheoses. He does not consign his figures either to heaven or hell. He does not consummate, nor end with a moral as in a fable. The last act leaves us in suspense. Will it end well or badly? Who can say? There is no end.

Here a reclining man looks at a seated woman. The painting has been called *La Boudeuse* (The Sulky Girl). Has a woman sulking in a garden ever been a subject for an artist? And how do we know she is sulking? It is the painting that fills us with wonder—the crinkle of black watered silk that echoes the rustling of the foliage; the blue of the water in the background; the blue and white of a sky subsiding with the setting of the sun. This elegant couple has left a palace or a theater to venture into a park.

Filmmakers, and especially Fellini, have depicted characters who leave some revels for a surprising encounter with the reality of trees, meadows, ponds, and find themselves able to harmonize with this world from which they seem so alienated. Hamlet could talk to a gravedigger. In Watteau, we are far from all romanticism and literature. A title like *La Boudeuse* stifles this painting and says nothing of the thousand harmonies linking the black dress and the leaves. *After the Fête* smothers it under intentions the painter never had. Watteau simply painted a couple in a park with a great distance between them.

All commentators on Watteau have employed musical comparisons, and to do so is not misleading. The formulas of language coarsen a creation that is all refinement, and, although purely pictorial, nonetheless purely human.

François Clouet
(French; before 1510–1572).
Portrait of Charles IX

Pierre Dumonstier
(French; c. 1550–1625).
Portrait of a Nobleman

sold it to the owners of a salmon fishery on the shores of the Caspian Sea. These mysterious wanderings ended in 1914 when the Hermitage acquired the work. Incidentally, we might mention that the last available Leonardo was acquired by the National Gallery in Washington from the Principality of Liechtenstein in 1967.

It was likewise for the Raphaels. The Hermitage owned only three, the *Alba Madonna*, purchased in 1836, and the *Holy Family* and the *Saint George and the Dragon* that had been part of the Crozat Collection. Persuading Count Conestabile of Perugia to sell his Madonna to a collection so far away was not easy, but the Russian emissary managed to overcome the count's objections and to obtain the export documents. The *Madonna Conestabile* remained in the czar's private apartments for ten years, before being placed in the museum in 1881.

The acquisition of a Fra Angelico fresco was another master stroke, one of many purchases of exceptional works that increased the attractions of the Hermitage. Museum buyers also watched Russian private collections, for the great fortunes were not stable enough to weather all difficulties and noblemen did not always keep their paintings.

The Hermitage bought seventy-five paintings from the Galitzin Collection and seven hundred from the Semenov Collection in 1886. The museum also received a certain number of paintings—Rembrandts, Tiepolos, Bouchers—too valuable to be used merely to decorate the walls of nearby imperial palaces. Thus, at the end of the nineteenth century and the beginning of the twentieth there was a partial consolidation of the artistic riches already present in Russia, and as a result the

Jacques Callot (French; 1592–1635). *Allegorical Car*

Nicolas Poussin (French; 1594–1665). *Achilles on Skyros*

museum's limitations were revealed. The machine put in motion some fifty years before had functioned very well, but as soon as it reached its full capacity, it arrived at the saturation point. Nothing had changed since the collections had first been organized according to Waagen's advice. The operation was a success, and there was nothing left to do except watch the circulation of visitors, dust the marbles, and take care of minor details. Newly acquired works went into the reserves or were shown in temporary exhibitions, for nothing was permitted to disturb the fine aesthetic system that had been set up. The Hermitage, the successful result of intelligence brought to bear on the conception of beauty born in Greece and renewed under Raphael, remained unchanged, definitive, behind its facade of a Roman villa stricken by gigantism. But then is not beauty said to be eternal?

It was at this time that French painting was overturning all the accepted rules. Not official French painting, of course, but the other kind which had not been admitted to fashionable exhibitions and had to be discovered by chance in a photographer's studio, on the walls of apartments rented for the occasion, and even at small, not quite reputable dealers. There were Russians who took pride in their love for this art, which they approached rather in the manner of Catherine II, who had wanted many paintings and claimed them greedily. Also like Catherine, they had no plan to assemble harmonious collections; they simply bought what they liked. In some twenty years, these men set up collections of such scope that in the Hermitage today the section devoted to nineteenth- and twentieth-century French painting is as large as that covering the history of French art of the fifteenth, sixteenth, seventeenth, and eighteenth centuries. Nor should we overlook some important examples of the Barbizon School and certain academic works once owned by the Kushelev, Sheremetiev, and Yusupov families. However, while these had been bought more out of propriety than passion, the other collections, although later to be divided between Moscow and Leningrad, still make clear the extravagant manner in which they had been acquired. Nobody buys some fifty Matisses, forty or so Picassos, fifteen of Marquet's works, a like number of works by Bonnard and Maurice Denis, or twenty-five Cézannes without having a passion for them. If we reconstruct the original collections by studying the catalogues of the two museums that house the works today, we may divine the personalities of these men. One of them, Morosov, liked the Impressionists and bought Monet, Renoir, Sisley, and Cézanne at a time when to have one of these masters on one's wall was a novelty and not an investment. He also indulged himself in a fine group of Gauguins. He was undoubtedly deeply gratified by the Impressionists, for he remained faithful in his later purchases to clear painting, dazzling color, and pleasant subjects. From Maurice Denis in 1908–9 he bought eleven huge paintings, each more than thirteen feet long, on the theme of Psyche. He commissioned three enormous panels on a Mediterranean theme from Bonnard in 1911. He bought a few Fauves (Derain, Friesz) but went no further than Matisse, stopping short of his more daring works.

The other collector, Shchukin, reveals a wider curiosity. His purchases literally followed the development of painting, even in those experiments that his contemporaries found it difficult to accept. He began with Forain, Carrière, Whistler, and even Charles Cottet, then moved on to the Impressionists. He bought their works, as he bought those of Gauguin and Van Gogh, but soon departed from his colleague Morosov, whose interest in the Nabis he did not share. He was enthusiastic about Derain when that artist was in his Cézannesque phase, and about Matisse, from whom he commissioned in 1908 a decoration for his dining room and in 1910 panels for the staircase landings of his

Jacques Bellange (French; fl. c. 1600–1617).
Study of a Female Figure

Jacques Foucquier (French; 17th century).   *Woody Landscape*

Jean-Baptiste Oudry
(French; 1686–1755).
The Hunt

Moscow residence. The paintings he hung in his home were so daring for the time as to be scarcely admissible. He went even further with Picasso, whom he followed faithfully in all his experiments, first buying Montmartre café scenes from the artist's early years in Paris, then sad silent works of the Blue Period, the violent images of the time of *Les Demoiselles d'Avignon*, and finally Analytic and Synthetic Cubist paintings. The range of his purchases covers the painter's career from the beginning of the century until 1914—the last picture was acquired shortly before the declaration of war.

There were probably other collectors of contemporary art in Russia, but the great names of the nobility had not gone beyond Dupré, Meissonier, Théodore Rousseau, Leibl, and Lembach. In a way, the aristocracy was afflicted with the same paralysis as the Hermitage itself. Guided by the aesthetic principles with which they had grown up, most of them avoided the phenomenon of renewal taking place in Paris. They often went to France, but clung to their own ways and remained isolated in a Parisian milieu that also rejected new ideas. Shchukin, being a free man, soon surrounded by young Moscow artists who admired his purchases, was able to understand what was new and fresh in Paris studios. And we must not overlook the fact that this collector of Picassos and Matisses also owned works from the past—by Guardi, Van Ostade, Lawrence, even the primitive Segno de Bonaventura. His modern collection was an act of faith.

One result, of course, is that the Hermitage has become even more unbalanced as a museum. It was already so, owing to the abundance of Dutch paintings that in their time had aroused the enthusiasm of Catherine II. But then what museum is not unbalanced? We imagine, separated by some 120 years, the two figures of the empress and the Moscow merchant, the first opening the history of the museum, the second closing its first chapter, and we see that they had at least one thing in common—the love of art.

ALL THE WEALTH OF RUSSIA

The Russians are reputed to be capricious and volatile, but they demonstrated a capacity for careful deliberation during the October Revolution. Damage to the buildings was minimal, the collections were not vandalized, and all that happened was the transfer to Moscow of the entire contents of the Hermitage and the Winter Palace. Then everything was brought back, and the curators began the huge task of sorting and cataloguing. In a single stroke, both the imperial and private collections had been nationalized, and they found themselves faced with an influx of works that exceeded all expectation. More than ten thousand paintings may have passed through their hands, and since many had never been previously indexed, everything had to be examined and classified. The next problem was what to do with them, whether to transform the palaces that had originally housed them into public museums. Although this made study more difficult by obliging the visitor to go all over the city to see the paintings that interested him, it was accepted. A museum of modern Western art was set up in Moscow by combining the Morosov and Shchukin collections, while the Stroganov Collection remained in its palace on the Moika Quay. This was nothing but a temporary solution, the goal being to assemble everything in one place.

One might have thought that, faced with such abundance, the Russians would have tried to divide it in such a way that the larger cities of the USSR would receive portions allowing each to set up a

Claude Gillot (French; 1673–1722). *Costumes for a Ballet*

Nicolas Lancret (French; 1690–1743). *A Young Gentleman*

museum worthy of its own importance. But this was not done. The Kiev Museum nationalized the collection of the Ukrainian collector Khanenko, but it is insufficient in many respects and there was nothing else. Leningrad thus retained its artistic preeminence, and only Moscow received special favor. The Moscow Museum, opened in 1912, had chiefly exhibited casts used to instruct students in the history of art, little enough for such a large city. Nor did the Soviets install a large museum such as any world capital should have. They simply added about eight hundred paintings of all periods and schools, which was all very well but in no way altered the prestige of the Hermitage. The latter was even strengthened, and it remains the only museum in Russia where one can receive a complete initiation into the history of art.

With the addition of the Winter Palace as room for expansion the museum began to thrive, taking what it needed from such existing public collections as the Academy of Fine Arts and the Russian Museum and skimming off the cream from the palaces and private homes of the city and its environs. Henceforth the museum was able to grow. Of the thousand and fifty rooms in the four adjoining palaces, it occupied three hundred, half of them for the exhibition of paintings, the rest for its other treasures. Leningrad has thus remained the focal point of foreign art that the czars had desired. Although it has changed its coat of arms, Russia remains a two-headed eagle, one of whose heads, Leningrad, faces the outside world and its past, while the other, Moscow, clings to tradition and to what has been or will be born under the new era.

François Boucher (French; 1703–1770).
Study of a Young Woman

Although history never repeats itself, the same phenomena sometimes produce similar reactions. Faced with an abundant concentration of works of art, the Soviets behaved like Nicholas I and decided to sell some of their treasures. They used two methods: public auctions and private transactions.

The many public sales were held principally in Berlin and Leipzig, with lavish catalogues reproducing all the works offered. In 1928, for example, at Rudolf Lepke's gallery in Berlin, nearly four hundred art objects—furniture, tapestries, paintings, sculpture, enamels, jewelry, clocks, and snuffboxes—said to be from the Hermitage and from the Mikhailovsky and Gatchina palaces were put up for sale. About one hundred paintings were included. Another hundred were sold at another Berlin sale in the same year. Three years later, the Soviets put the Stroganov Collection up for auction at Lepke's. There were one hundred and ten paintings, in addition to furniture, ivories, vases, plates, and bronzes. Engravings (about forty-five hundred prints) and drawings were sold in Leipzig. Bronzes and paintings were also auctioned off in Vienna.

It is not unusual for the seller at a public auction to withdraw works from the bidding. The Soviet Union acted likewise, withholding from the Stroganov sale a famous Poussin, the *Rest on the Flight into Egypt*, which had been offered as part of the collection. The painting went back to Leningrad and can still be seen at the Hermitage.

The Hermitage did not lose irreplaceable items by these public sales. On the other hand, the transactions that took place behind the scenes between Russian officials and foreign collectors ended by depriving the museum of some real masterpieces. It happened as follows: Gulbenkian, the oil magnate, had facilitated for the USSR the exportation of its oil, and the Russians asked how they could express their thanks. Aware of the Soviet public sales in Germany, Gulbenkian suggested that he might perhaps be allowed to buy certain works directly. A German expert, Francis Matthiessen, was called to Leningrad in 1929 to evaluate the hundred major paintings in the Hermitage. From the list compiled by the expert (who stressed that no great museum should ever give up such works at any price), the oil magnate was invited to choose. Gulbenkian acquired a number of paintings, six of which, by Rembrandt, Rubens, Hubert Robert, and Dirk Bouts, are now in the Gulbenkian Foundation in Portugal.

Once the ice had been broken, an international gallery contacted the Russians through Matthiessen and acquired thirty-one paintings for Andrew Mellon, United States Secretary of the Treasury and founder of the National Gallery in Washington. These paintings—by Raphael, Botticelli, Titian, Veronese, Van Eyck, Velázquez, Van Dyck, Rembrandt, and Frans Hals—are now in the National Gallery with the rest of the Mellon Collection. And there were other departures: a Watteau went to the Metropolitan Museum of Art in New York, some Tiepolos to the Melbourne Museum and the Musée Cognacq-Jay in Paris.

Gabriel de Saint-Aubin (French; 1724–1780).
Games in the Park

Jean-Baptiste Greuze (French; 1725–1805).
Study of a Woman

Hubert Robert (French; 1733–1808).
Villa Madama

These were the most serious losses. The Hermitage now has no painting by Van Eyck, and the two small Botticelli panels that remain do not compensate for the loss of that artist's *Adoration of the Magi*.

Such transfers should remind us of the fate of certain works. Let us follow, for example, the course of Raphael's *Saint George and the Dragon*, which Mellon obtained from the Hermitage. It had been given to King Henry VII of England, and remained a crown possession until Cromwell beheaded Charles I in 1649. The Roundheads sold the king's property and the Raphael went to France. It remained there until the Revolution, when it was purchased by Catherine II. The Russian Revolutionaries in turn sold the work to Andrew Mellon. Such travels may be disconcerting but can be taken more philosophically by reading a passage from the will of Edmond de Goncourt: "It is my wish that . . . the works of art that brought me so much happiness in life escape the cold tomb of a museum and the stupid gaze of indifferent passers-by, and I ask that they be dispersed under the blows of the auctioneer's gavel, so that the pleasure I felt in their acquisition be passed on to an heir with tastes like mine." Such are the desires that surround a work of art. We envy those who possess them and are happy to possess them ourselves. Yet, when we have hated the previous owner, something of that hatred attaches to his belongings even though he has lost them, and if we are destitute, we exchange them gladly for the things we need. This is what the Russians did. Furthermore, they sold collections of icons in Zurich, Paris, and London.

These sales did not go unprotested. Ten years after the end of World War I, Russian émigrés saw the USSR offer paintings and art objects that they considered property of which they had been illegally stripped. Legal summonses were served at the auctions; pamphlets were distributed: *Kaufe kein enteignetes Gut* ("Do Not Buy Expropriated Goods"). These efforts had little effect on sales. The courts frequently declared themselves incompetent, and governments showed no hesitation in choosing between the weakness of the émigrés and the strength of the Soviet government. As recently as July, 1954, when thirty-seven Picassos from the museums of Leningrad and Moscow were to be exhibited in Paris, Sergei Shchukin's daughter tried to get an order from the French courts to seize the paintings. All in vain—the paintings went back to Russia, and another exhibition was substituted. Shchukin himself had declared before his death that, although he regretted the loss of his paintings, he had always intended them for a museum, and this is perhaps the most sensible conclusion that anyone can draw half a century after the nationalization of the collections.

A work of art is undoubtedly an asset that can be calculated in money on those art stock exchanges that in effect are constituted by auctioneers' offices. Yet each owner knows, somehow, that he is never more than a trustee. Sooner or later, the work is promised to a museum, where it will be shown to those who can best appreciate it. The movement is irresistible, and one hears cries of alarm from the dealers—soon they will have nothing to sell or at least nothing good.

When, in 1965, one hundred French paintings from Soviet collections were shown in Bordeaux and Paris, the ensuing polemics were purely aesthetic. If there were still heirs of the former owners, they no longer thought to assert their claims. This was due, of course, to the dissolution of rancor, but also to the opinion that the Soviets make good use of their art, even if they do not show it all. Few museums lend their masterpieces for foreign exhibition as willingly as the Hermitage. One is never more than a trustee.

THE MUSEUM MAKERS

Among the "trustees" who acquired such wealth in the two hundred years between the purchase of Rembrandt's *David's Farewell to Jonathan* in 1716 and the successful Bolshevik attack on the Winter Palace on October 25, 1917, are some particularly picturesque figures, so ennobled by their possessions that one is tempted to absolve them of all sin because they loved such-and-such a painting, drawing, or etching. Having followed the growth of the collections and spoken at length of the impassioned collectors Shchukin and Morosov, we should perhaps return to the men and women to whom we are indebted for making a trip to Leningrad the occasion to rediscover centuries of European painting. We can thus follow the manner in which the concept of art evolved alongside the history of the Hermitage.

As for Peter the Great, we can suppose that he reacted to Dutch and French paintings as he did to methods of mining or shipbuilding—with the fascination of a man confronted by a cultural level that seems to him ideal and which he accepts without reservations. He posed for the portraitists Oudry, Largillière, and Rigaud. It is significant that he wished to witness the creation of Nattier's *The Battle of Poltava*, in which the painter represented him galloping amid the cannon bursts and pointing out the action to the viewer. It is no less significant that he did not repeat the experience of being represented allegorically, as Jacopo Amigoni, who had never seen him, had painted him on commission from the Russian ambassador to London. Peter the Great went wherever he could, stopping at the edge of the ridiculous; still, he did not reject this transfiguration into an ideal that was surely not his own. He had admired its effectiveness on a visit to Versailles, where he paid less attention to the child Louis XV, who received him, than to the glorification of Louis XIV.

His daughter Elizabeth was less of a collector than her successor, Catherine II. Although she posed for such artists as Tocqué and Lagrenée, she was more interested in training painters than in having herself painted. She remembered that her father had wanted Oudry and Nattier to come to Russia and repeated his request. Although nothing came of this effort, she distinguished herself as a ruler by founding the Academy of Fine Arts.

Catherine II never forgot her education as a German princess. Her interests lay entirely in Western Europe, where her power had no difficulty in bringing home to intellectuals how little their own governments appreciated them. She acted as an imposing lever that guaranteed their authority, and they gave her in return the intellectual grace that she had always dreamed of. Curiously enough, she made good use of writers as intermediaries between painters, paintings, and herself. She was always quite satisfied with reports she received, never left Russia, purchased everything abroad, and never saw anything she had bought until it arrived at the palace. She posed for artists who lived in or passed through Saint Petersburg—Roslin, Fontebasso, Virgilius Erichsen, Richard Brompton, Johann Baptist Lampi. Despite her enormous correspondence with the outside world, Catherine did not commission very many works. She ordered from Reynolds, Chardin, Vien, Casanova, Van Loo, De Machy, and Angelica Kauffmann, but perhaps basically she was simply playing the role of a lady who suddenly has the means to acquire marvels, to own what her previous circumstances had not accorded her before. She was more at home in the company of writers than in that of artists, and she was quite humble about her art treasures, knowing that she did not fully appreciate their beauty. And she was happy to heed the lessons given by her friends "in the business." This is not the least engaging aspect of Catherine's career as a collector.

Catherine's remark upon receiving a shipment of paintings from Paris has often been quoted: "Only the mice and I can admire all this!" Not everybody was permitted entrance into the building that was then really her private hermitage, but her collections had curators, usually painters capable of repairing the damages caused by transportation. During her reign, the president of the Chamber of Commerce, Count Munich, prepared and published a critical catalogue, which was quite competent according to those who have read it. Thus, Catherine II had a team to take care of her purchases, and the masterpieces that came to Saint Petersburg were properly handled. In addition, she wished to stimulate a love of art among young people. She acquired the Shuvalov Collection for the Academy, where she also placed a number of paintings from her own collections. This concern corrects somewhat the impression of avidity often suggested by the letters in which she speaks of her paintings.

While he was still a grand duke, her son Paul I and his wife traveled through Europe, visiting Vienna, Rome, and Paris, where Paul was impressed by the architectural projects of Claude-Nicolas Ledoux. Their visit to Venice left its trace in painting, for Francesco Guardi painted a series of pictures of the festivities given in honor of the couple, traveling as the Comte and Comtesse du Nord —a concert, an evening at the theater, a parade of allegorical floats, and so on. The future czar did not ask for copies of these works, and they remained in Italy or were purchased by those zealous collectors of Venetian painting, the English. Paul was interested in Greuze, Vernet, and Hubert Robert, and purchased some of their work, and we know that he considered bringing his mother a Pompeo Batoni as a gift from Rome. But his principal contribution to the history of the Hermitage was his removal of a number of pictures to his nearby residences, the Pavlovsk, Gatchina, and Mikhailovsky palaces.

Alexander I increased the collections by acquiring early works, including 118 pictures from the

PABLO PICASSO (Spanish; 1881–1973)
Dryad

Painted in 1908

Oil on canvas, 72 7/8 × 42 1/2"

Catalogue No. 7704.   Formerly Shchukin Collection

Picasso painted this nude among the trees in 1908. He had been settled in Paris for four years and was perhaps influenced by the commemorative exhibition for Cézanne (who had died in 1906) at the Salon d'Automne in 1907. Do we see here the precept of Cézanne's *Bathers*? The history of painting abounds in examples of the geometrization of forms, from Uccello to Cambiaso and Vermeer.

Compared to *Les Demoiselles d'Avignon,* this work seems almost Classical, more solidly constructed, less exuberant in color. And, while the *Demoiselles* contains a new unity, the *Dryad* is limited to the exploration of one of the many ideas revealed in the larger painting. It is more modest in its ambitions, and constitutes one stage in the methodical exploitation of an idea. There were to be others, and the Hermitage has examples in *Woman with a Fan* (1908) and *Queen Isabeau* (1909). Picasso's approach to Cubism is characteristically personal. He depended less than his colleagues on still life and landscape, and more on the portrait, a realm in which it is easier to offend human sensibilities—which is not to say that we should see in Picasso either a systematic *provocateur* or the most reasonable of artists.

Empress Josephine's collection at Malmaison. He had the intelligence to bring to Saint Petersburg what had previously been lacking such as Spanish paintings, thirty of which he bought at the sale of the Godoy Collection. He was likewise astute enough to employ the talents of such an exceptional man as Dominique Vivant Denon, who was as successful as an archaeologist in Egypt, a writer of *contes galants*, and an organizer of public fêtes, as he was in administering the fabulous collections gathered all across Europe by Napoleon's armies. Denon found some masterpieces for the czar. Alexander I also posed for the artists who visited Saint Petersburg—Voille, Vigée-Lebrun, Mosnier, and Krüger—and sat for Gérard in Paris.

For Alexander, the collection was primarily a patrimony. He admired it and added to it, but found it too distinctly marked by Catherine. Hence, he had it systematically arranged by professionals, and this was doubtless the first step in the long slow process of nationalization. This process is generally explained by the progressive opening of the royal possessions to lovers of art, as the demands of a growing public gradually forced open all the doors of private domains. One might also stress the fact that when the patrimony is so large (2,658 paintings in 1785, 3,996 at the beginning of the next century) it is almost crushing. Unless the heir to such an estate is passionately fond of art and a visual glutton, he necessarily becomes alienated from such abundance and feels the need to turn its administration over to specialists. Under Alexander I, the Hermitage collection was organized. The curator Labensky set up a restoration studio and a school for training restorers who specialized in the transfer of paintings from wood to canvas, a delicate operation that saved many works.

Finally, it was Alexander's idea to open special rooms in the Hermitage to celebrate the victory of Russia and her allies over Napoleon. This use of painting for the glorification of heroes was not a new idea, but it took on new life and spread across Europe. Thus Windsor has its Waterloo Chamber, Vienna its Army Museum. Louis-Philippe installed a gallery at Versailles to celebrate French victories from the Crusades (depicted by Delacroix) to 1830. But, unlike the Versailles Museum, which was open to the public (its purpose being to act as a historical catalyst for the different classes of French society), the National War Gallery in Saint Petersburg remained a very private place, reserved for the use of the Court; entrance was by invitation only.

La Harpe, Alexander's Swiss tutor, of course exaggerated when he remarked of his pupil: "The most incredulous had to admit that he was one of those rare specimens of humanity who appear once every thousand years." But Alexander was truly to organize his collections as a museum should be organized.

Nicholas I inaugurated the War Gallery prepared by his predecessor. There is something symbolic in this. The new emperor carried to conclusion the indications laid down by Alexander I, at least in the sphere of the fine arts. This is in accord with what we know of the orderly disposition of that sovereign who wanted a country run on the principles of absolute monarchy, but not paralyzed by them. It was thus Nicholas who built an up-to-date museum, put it in order, and decided, like the excellent mathematician that he was, that one out of every four of the catalogued forty-five hundred paintings could be disposed of. Shocking though this may seem, an abundance of mediocre paintings undoubtedly made it necessary.

Alexander II stands out for his acquisition of major works by such painters as Raphael and Leonardo, and for allowing his curators to work more and more toward perfecting the museum, now finally a public one. During his reign, the collections passed even more distinctly from the status of crown possessions to that of national property. The museum had ended by finding its autonomy within the great complex of palaces.

Alexander III acquired the Galitzin Museum of 102 paintings. Nicholas II opened the Russian Museum, which again separated foreign painting from Russian works.

We cannot limit this rapid enumeration of those who created the Hermitage only to the czars. Seventy years after the 1854 sale (which left 3,333 paintings in the museum and the imperial residences), the collections contained more than 8,000 works. Thus, private collections have contributed more to the wealth of the Hermitage than imperial collections. The ostentation of Russian travelers in Europe, and their avidity for art, led to a kind of legend about the "boyar" buying paintings by the score or the hundred—it parallels that of the footloose American in Montparnasse between the two world wars. Such a myth clearly implied certain reservations on the quality of taste of these huge appetites that did not buy in the same cautious manner as the natives. This is understandable, the travelers being pressed for time and freed by the capacity of their pocketbooks. Their purchases were also the easiest way to gain entry into the society they wished to seduce, as well as proof, on their return to Russia, of the success of their trip. Shuvalov, for example, settled in Rome in 1767, and had himself painted by the fashionable artist, Pompeo Batoni. Then he went to Paris, where Greuze painted his portrait and that of his wife. He was deeply interested in the works of Hubert Robert and bought many of his paintings, but he also bought Poussins, a Watteau from the Horace Walpole Collection, and works by Jordaens, Rubens, and Cranach. Vorontzov started collecting in Italy in 1745, Sheremetiev in 1758. Stroganov resided in both Italy and France, and the catalogue of his collection went from Dirk Bouts to Reynolds, and included Botticelli. Yusupov was said to be richer than the czar, and had his own theater company, ballet, and orchestra. His gallery of paintings, by Lorrain, Boucher, Corot, Poussin, and David, matched his fortune. Scattered throughout numerous family palaces (the Yusupovs had four in Petrograd and three in Moscow), and seldom catalogued, these incredible treasures remained unknown. Russia seemed a kind of forest into which many masterpieces vanished, an unfathomed region where these Russian Croesuses dispersed their treasures in enchanted caves.

This explains the general astonishment that greeted the appearance in 1909 of a completely unknown Leonardo da Vinci, and in 1922 of a "lost" Poussin, which was found in the reserves of the Academy of Fine Arts. The Soviet collections have not yet yielded up all their surprises. But the enormous task of inventory and publication undertaken by the Hermitage staff will surely end by rendering futile any inquiry by art historians on the track of a vanished work. They will no longer wonder whether a lost painting may still be hidden in the Russian maze. Europe will be less and less cut off from the works that were carried off by the Russian lovers of art. And what is now being done for the art of former times will soon be done for that of our own.

There is one more lesson to be drawn from the history of the Hermitage. In this palace, as in all the other gigantic constructions once built for them, princes no longer live. Art has taken their place, imposing its own laws where they once ruled the country. Teams of specialists spare nothing to provide good lighting and proper atmospheric conditions. You who are collectors know that sooner or later it will not be your descendants that people will come to your homes to see, but your pictures. So beware of painting. In Leningrad, the museum will end by occupying all the Hermitages.

The COLORPLATES

FILIPPINO LIPPI (Italian; c. 1457–1504)

Adoration

Undated

Tempera on wood transferred to copper, diameter 20 7/8"

Catalogue No. 287.   Formerly Stroganov Collection

Filippino Lippi worked in both Rome and Florence. It was he who had the difficult task of completing the fresco decorations begun by Masolino di Panicale and Masaccio in the Brancacci Chapel of the Florentine Church of Santa Maria del Carmine. It was he who painted the Strozzi Chapel in Santa Maria Novella. The old Gothic interior was completely transformed, repainted with architectural motifs such as are found in Pompeian frescoes—columns, lifelike statues, fantastic grotesques, in a clear light that seems to open the wall upon an antique sky. It is hard to believe that these airy, fanciful decorations were almost contemporary with Leonardo da Vinci's *Last Supper.*

In contrast to the earthy, monumental (one is tempted to say "mineral," since in Florence marble is the most important stone) quality in the work of his father, Filippo Lippi, the son Filippino's style is nervous, graceful, a bit superficial perhaps, but one that pleased his time by its erudite references ("men, weapons, trophies, urns, helmets," as Vasari noted with interest), made without insistence, and which hold our attention today by their elegance.

Here, Filippino Lippi displays other tendencies. This is no longer entertaining decoration but a withdrawal into the self. This picture represents the introduction of melancholy into an outmoded formula. For in painting this *Adoration* the artist, who had been a pupil of Botticelli, is far from following him in his rather precious theatricality, and instead has surely remembered similar pictures by his father Filippo (now to be seen in the Uffizi and the Berlin museums). He has adhered to the rules, but the times have changed. He keeps the poses and costumes, but he disposes of the heavy halos, relinquishes the whole display of rocks, rivers, and forests that represent the different aspects of the world, and renounces the assemblies of angels and the figure of God leaning over a heavenly balcony to survey the scene.

He who had introduced the enchanting forms of the antique into religious art here imparts to the Christian scene something of the smiling and earthly simplicity that the painters of the School of Cologne were expressing at the same time, as well as that natural landscape contributed by artists of the Low Countries. The true note is struck by the yellow sunlight obscured by some storm clouds, and by the opening of the picture on the ideal vanishing point of the perspective—the infinite sea.

But the mother of Christ is not a chatelaine from the banks of the Rhine playing with her newborn infant in a closed garden. She is separated from the world not by a wall but by a marble balustrade, highly useful for the order of the composition, marvelous for the setting itself, and which may well have the symbolic significance that we find in the *Allegory of the Tree of Life* by Filippino's contemporary Giovanni Bellini (c. 1430–1516).

LEONARDO DA VINCI (Italian; 1452–1519)

Benois Madonna

Painted about 1478
Oil on wood transferred to canvas, 19 1/4 × 12 1/4"
Catalogue No. 2773.   Formerly Benois Collection

The sudden appearance in 1909 of this unknown and forgotten painting at the exhibition in Petrograd of masterworks from Russian private collections came as a great surprise. The work was presented without the slightest suggestion as to its possible creator, but critical opinion immediately proposed the name of Leonardo da Vinci. Historians recalled an entry in the artist's notebooks: "1478. I began two Virgin Marys." If one of these was the *Madonna with the Carnation* in Munich, then the second was undoubtedly the painting from the Benois Collection. It was a fabulous discovery. For, although variants and copies existed, the quality of this version was impressive enough to convince most, if not all, art historians that it was a major work by Leonardo.

It is undoubtedly a youthful work without the complexity, the symbolic theatricality, of more ambitious paintings, but it testifies to the sense of happiness that Leonardo would later impart to the *Virgin and Child with Saint Anne* now in the Louvre. There is a difference, however—here the feminine model has not yet become fixed in abstraction. This young woman still belongs to the world and not to that pure sphere where life is sublimated to spirituality. Still almost a child herself, she plays with her infant as did very young mothers of Leonardo's time. She has a freshness that Leonardo was to abandon little by little. Hers is not the smile of a goddess, but of a woman.

A very complex construction accompanies this naturalness. Virgin and Child are defined in balanced rhythms, their tempo imparted by the drapery at the bottom. The movement rises into the arms of the two figures, passes to the neckline of the blouse, and culminates in a triangle enclosing the two heads, while the keystone of the window arch reverses the movement and sends it back toward the bottom whence it came. This is an extremely dynamic work and, at the same time, a creation enclosed upon itself.

LEONARDO DA VINCI (Italian; 1452–1519)
Madonna Litta

Painted about 1490

Tempera on wood transferred to canvas, 16 1/2 × 13"

Catalogue No. 249.   Purchased from Duke Antonio Litta of Milan, 1865

Between the Benois and Litta Madonnas lies the difference between what is natural and what is simulated. Leonardo here moves into another dimension in which all appearances have been pondered and reconstructed, and where forceful unity of style triumphs over the more or less irregular accents taken from life. The painting moreover achieves monumental simplicity. The artist no longer needs folds, rumpled drapery, rhythms held in place with difficulty by strict construction. Symmetry reigns, forms blossom, and colors increase in intensity to reach their maximum strength. In the blues of cloak and sky, the red of the blouse, the painter uses all the resources of his palette.

Much discussion has revolved around this painting. It has been attributed successively to Luini, Jacopo del Conti, Ambrogio da Predis, d'Oggiono, Boltraffio, and others, including Leonardo, but with the stipulation that his was not the only hand. Clearly, historians are disturbed by something in this work, but we might add that unanimously accepted Leonardos are very rare. This one, however, seems guaranteed by a touching drawing in the Louvre of a woman with bent head—the same likeness, with a nose slightly too long, eyes lowered, and a faintly bitter mouth. The painting idealizes these features, making them smooth and pure, while keeping their vulnerability, for the painted Madonna has the face of the woman in the drawing. Furthermore, the works of his disciples Melzi, Luini, Da Predis, and the others never attain this stature and are often Leonardesque bodies without the formal density that gives strength to his work. It is strange, besides, that our conception of Leonardo should remain attached to his aesthetic principles, yet continue to be so captious about what he might or might not have done with his hands. How is one to reconcile the image of the great, lonely, inventive genius, who upset all the artistic thought of his time, with that of the head of a workshop, the master of a business, who had to parcel out his work?

We may well wonder why critics persisted in refusing to attribute this work to Leonardo. One of the chief reasons may be that most of his works were painted in oil, in the new process taken over from Northern artists. The old Italian tempera technique used for this Madonna results, necessarily, in more brilliance than flexibility and perhaps explains why the facial color is not so soft as we might expect. But nothing precludes the desire of the artist to try his style in an old technique, prepared to relinquish it once the experiment was over.

CIMA DA CONEGLIANO (Italian; c. 1459–1517/18)
Annunciation

Painted in 1495

Oil and tempera on wood transferred to canvas, 53 5/8 × 42 1/8"

Catalogue No. 256.   Formerly Galitzin Collection

The great lion of Saint Mark, measuring fifteen feet in length, that greets visitors to the Ca' d'Oro in Venice is by Cima da Conegliano. Many Madonnas that one would think were by Giovanni Bellini are likewise Cima's, and in some of the background landscapes there is an echo of Giorgione's manner of evoking the mystery of nature. There are also Oriental scenes—Venice pretending to recognize itself in the exotic—painted in the style of Gentile Bellini, and large religious works that one would attribute to Francia. And there are retables with gold backgrounds like those of Alvise Vivarini. We might well ask if there is anything personal or interesting in this painter, whom Vasari presented simply as a pupil of Giovanni Bellini. His diverse styles suggest so many references that it is not unreasonable to describe him as a follower.

It is true that Cima da Conegliano lived in a period of transition. He was one of a generation of artists that found it hard to admit that the art of gilded retables was undergoing an aesthetic revolution. They were surprised at being able to carry it forward, and confident enough that they could control it. This picture, the central panel of a screen painted for the Crocicchieri Church in Venice (the side panels representing Saint Mark and Saint Sebastian are in the National Gallery in London), dispenses with the gold background, replacing it with a polychrome landscape and interior. This calls for variety, and we have on one side sky, hills, and architecture, and on the other the shadow of a door where the brilliance of the reds and blues imparts a new strength to the silence. While the angel advances with a light step that touches the ground in only a trace of earthly reality, Cima discloses all the resources of painting, and finds a whole technique of animation in the openings and closings of perspective planes at the bottom of the picture.

What is admirable about him is that he did not let himself be overcome by any formula, and was able to go from lively narrative to stable and monumental form with an ease that always permitted an original talent to emerge, free of aesthetic entanglements. Cima da Conegliano's career is not without interest in the age of aesthetic mutations in which we live. He, too, lived many adventures of the spirit. And he survived them.

TITIAN (Italian; 1477/87–1576)
Portrait of a Young Woman

Painted about 1530
Oil on canvas, 38 × 29 1/2"
Catalogue No. 71.   Formerly Crozat Collection

It was in the sixteenth century that nudity entered into the pictures of all European schools of art. Baldung Grien, Cranach, the Fontainebleau artists and François Clouet in France, the Dutchman Glotzius, Hans van Aachen, and Heintz and Spranger at the court of Prague—all painted voluptuous creatures. But the painters all took the precaution of justifying their delight in beautiful flesh by the addition of some symbolic accessory—a quiver for Diana, a serpent for Cleopatra, a winged child for Venus—that displaced the subject and permitted a prince to preserve his propriety when these exposed ladies hung on the walls of his palace.

Titian here offers no excuse at all, no Biblical, mythological, or allegorical pretext. Thus he has no need of action, of the animation required by narrative. This woman is merely a woman, neither a Lucretia covering herself modestly, nor a Salome disrobing to dance. She is the reality of flesh, highlighted by the state of being partially disrobed. She takes her pose as for a portrait, like Isabella d'Este or the painter's daughter Laura. She keeps on her hat, the kind of hat perhaps worn on the streets of Venice but never seen in Titian's other paintings, and gravely waits in this temporary state of seminudity.

The catalogue of the Crozat Collection describes this work as "the portrait of a Venetian woman with a toque, a feather, and two arms, to the waist." She is recognizable as the model who posed for the *Venus of Urbino* in the Uffizi and for *La Bella* in the Pitti Palace. There is a comparable version without the plumed hat, but with more furs and one bare breast, in Vienna, for which the catalogue suggests the dates 1535–37.

Did the painter ever offer this work for sale? We would like to believe that he kept it for himself, for it is such an amorous and uncomplacent dialogue, a creation for the intimacy of a love affair.

GIORGIONE (Italian; c. 1478–1510)
Judith

Painted before 1508
Oil on wood transferred to canvas, 56 3/4 × 26 1/4"
Catalogue No. 95.   Formerly Crozat Collection

Everything about this Judith is perfection. Hair smoothly arranged, eyes lowered, she is a bit hampered by the heavy sword required for the pose and holds it with obvious clumsiness, like somebody armed with a weapon he does not know how to use. She places her pretty foot on the head— its eyes are closed, and the blood that spurted from it shortly before has been washed away—but she does not press too hard. One might say that she is a sister of those Virgins of Tiepolo who stand with one light foot on the globe or absentmindedly triumph over a serpent representing Evil. Another Judith, from Botticelli's workshop, hangs in the Uffizi. A dreamy young woman moves through the countryside, holding a saber in one hand and an olive branch in the other. A serving woman follows her, carrying the head of Holofernes in a basket on her own head.

The Giorgione *Judith*, when it belonged to Crozat, was taken for a Raphael, and there are actual resemblances in the crystalline perfection of the work. One does not, however, find in Raphael figures comparable to this one, completely self-enclosed, without a glance for the spectator, entirely absorbed in its own triumph and careless of the effect it produces. A Raphael would perhaps be more explicit than this painting, less monumental, and at the same time less fastidiously subtle.

When we think of the works accredited to Giorgione—the *Madonna of Castelfranco*, the *Three Philosophers* in Vienna, the *Tempest* in Venice, the *Venus* in Dresden—we can understand Mariette's uneasiness early in the eighteenth century over the attribution of this painting to Raphael. Such would be to stretch too much the recognized purity of that master. The most striking and novel features here are perhaps the silence that is evoked so that life may be better heard, and the manner of placing the tensions of the work on invisible threads, thus raising a structure as transparent as it is indestructible, where the least tremor takes on a formidable strength, and where the presence of mortals, draperies, grass, trees, attains a value all the more sublime because of a scrupulously respected realism.

This *Judith* retains from the medieval something of the appearance of a retable panel. But what a metamorphosis from the time when figures were surrounded by incised gold!

It is usually described as a youthful work. But if Giorgione's youth is represented by the *Judgment of Solomon* in the Uffizi, then this painting is surely contemporary with the *Madonna of Castelfranco*, which is far from the work of a beginner.

RAPHAEL (Italian; 1483–1520)
Madonna Conestabile

Painted about 1500

Tempera on wood transferred to canvas, 7 × 7 1/8"

Catalogue No. 252.   Formerly Conestabile Collection, Perugia

Scholars place this early work by Raphael between the years 1500 and 1504. The painting seems quite peaceful for the creation of a young man. If we look in it for something that foreshadows the artist's future, we find only a kind of recoil in relation to other figures painted by Perugino during this period—the Uffizi *Mary Magdalene*, for example, a much more finished painting in which the brushwork is hidden behind perfection of skin texture and polished fingernails. Indeed, it is perhaps here that Raphael's youthful opposition to his master appears. He proves that he is a painter who loves color and sees no need to hide his brushstrokes. Furthermore, this Madonna and Child is not so very far removed from the modesty of the Primitives. Some accents in the blue of the cloak, the transparency of a white veil on the red robe—we are not far from the muted flat colors of the past.

The landscape, too, is almost naive in its silence, in the little it says about itself. Raphael, however, adds a personal touch in the huge icy mountain rising on the right. Yet there is something more, the grace of the Child's body, rendered with an admirable economy of means—a few shadows. And the structuring of the bone of the nose, so subtly accomplished and so touching. This is, in a sense, the prototype of the sweet, beautiful Madonnas who brought fame to Raphael, and earned him the reproach of insipidity from those who pass by his paintings too rapidly, being drawn more to violence than to delicacy. Delacroix gave a very just definition of Raphael's grace: "It is an elegance in which the model has no part, a chaste verve, if one can call it that, an earthly manifestation of a soul that converses with the gods."

ANDREA DEL SARTO (Italian; 1486–1561)
Virgin and Child with Saints Catherine, Elizabeth, and John the Baptist

Painted about 1519

Oil on wood transferred to canvas, 40 1/8 × 31 1/2"

Catalogue No. 62.   Formerly Malmaison Collection of the Empress Josephine

Vasari describes Andrea del Sarto as a weak man, overly concerned with his wife, unable to seize the opportunity offered him in France by Francis I, and exploited by patrons throughout his life. This biography again employs the leitmotif the historian used each time he encountered an exceptional and unorthodox talent. "He was naturally gifted with so sweet and graceful a manner of drawing, so warm and easy a sense of color in both frescoes and oil paintings that, had he lived in Rome, he would have surpassed all the artists of his time." Vasari stresses the word "sweetness," using it several times. Finally, returning to the subject of the painter's great love, Vasari writes that he never painted a woman's head without using his wife as the model, which perhaps explains the similarity of features of the Virgin and Saint Catherine in this painting.

Actually, one should approach Andrea del Sarto without aesthetic theories. Once we remember that Raphael was three years his senior, and Pontormo six years his junior, we can place him better in this very short, disturbed period, full of contrary tendencies, to which his relationship was less theoretical than pictorial. Andrea del Sarto was sensitive to the charms of rising Mannerism, but did not let himself be totally caught up in it. At the same time he wished to go beyond strict Classicism.

He found his fulfillment in color. If his paintings escape systems and words, it is because they are basically extremely subtle interplays of colors, works of such delicate nuance that it is difficult to describe them verbally. Here, perhaps, this is accomplished at the expense of the personages, in whom we do not really believe, for with their empty eyes and frozen smiles they do not succeed in moving us. With all due allowance for the passage of time that has perhaps removed a little of the strength found in comparable works like the *Madonna of the Harpies* in the Uffizi, it may be that if these women appear to have so little connection with each other, it is because they express primarily the sweetness of painting.

PELLEGRINO TIBALDI (Italian; 1527–1596)
Holy Family with Saint Elizabeth

Undated

Oil on slate, 17 × 12"

Catalogue No. 128.   Formerly Crozat Collection

With what derisive names critics frequently baptize new movements in art! Is there not something pejorative in the terms Fauvism and Cubism, and did not the works themselves deserve to be called by a name that did not ridicule them? As for Mannerism, it immediately suggests "mannered." Scholars have seen in these sixteenth-century artists a frantic search for originality, a determination to discard the rules by accentuating rhythm and above all by playing with color as an independent element of expression, which ended by destroying the nice equilibrium extolled by the academicians. Hence they have often disregarded valuable masters on the pretext that they had avoided the arduous path on which their true qualities could have been judged. Now these artists are being rediscovered, among them Pellegrino Tibaldi, who enjoyed a successful career in Italy, from Bologna to Rome and Ferrara, before being invited to Spain by Philip II to decorate the Escorial. He was employed there with Federico Zuccaro and Luca Cambiaso; today guidebooks to the palace still reproach the artist and his Italian friends for an excessive use of color.

To be sure, some Mannerists, including Tibaldi, clung to the aesthetic principles of Michelangelo, but with considerable independence. They took from the master only his nervous rhythm, his use of perspective to create a surprising and undulating design in the most familiar forms. The basic elements were old, the spirit new, manifesting itself by its way of employing the full strength of color in large open areas. The painting becomes hollowed out, receding endlessly before the eye of the spectator. Here Tibaldi imposes a new vision of antiquity. This is not archaeological research, but a poetic fantasy, as we see in this very theatrical grouping where the figures are more separated than united, posed with a great display of ambiguous forms (such as the kind of shell or mother-of-pearl mouth beneath the Virgin) on the stage of an ancient amphitheater that is less a restoration than a reinvention.

The work, when it belonged to Crozat, was listed as a Parmigianino and called *Virgin and Child with Saint John.*

ANNIBALE CARRACCI (Italian; 1560–1609)
Self-Portrait

Painted about 1590
Oil on canvas, 17 × 12"
Catalogue No. 148.   Formerly Crozat Collection

One thinks of the work of Annibale Carracci perhaps a little too much in terms of the Accademia degli Incamminati, which he founded with his brother Agostino and cousin Ludovico in 1585. And it is obviously convenient to refer to the notion of a group with all the new ideas that it put into circulation. Certainly much of seventeenth-century painting derives from the Carracci; but by making these painters the source for the future of art, and showing how, in them, a vigorous idea of Classicism asserts itself in opposition to Mannerism, we arrive at an overly tempting balance of forces. We forget how these deep tendencies were intertwined, and if we separate the works into beautifully balanced allegories—realistic pictures like the *Butcher's Shop* in Oxford, noble landscapes, and certain humorous fantasies—we may overlook this exceptional painting, which is clearly not easy to classify.

The work is as astonishing as the self-portrait by Parmigianino, painted some sixty years earlier and showing the artist's reflection in a convex mirror—his reply to the distortions generally used for fantastic effects. In his own case, Annibale Carracci chose to paint the portrait of his portrait, to show himself as the painter of a painter. Everything is there, a small dog in one corner, the palette in another (to be looked at closely by anyone interested in the techniques of the masters), and with a mysterious silhouette standing before an equally mysterious window.

The painting poses an artistic problem that goes beyond historical formulas. Not easily reduced to the aesthetic principles attributed to the painter, it remains outside to such an extent that, despite its originality, nobody has imitated it. The idea never seems to have been taken up again. And yet, it may have been stronger than all the theories that can pass through the head of an artist.

CARAVAGGIO (Italian; 1573–1610)
Lute Player

Painted about 1594
Oil on canvas, 37 × 47″
Catalogue No. 45.   Formerly Giustiniani Collection

Giovanni Baglione, writing in 1642, described this as a work "painted for Cardinal del Monte . . . a youth playing the lute, very lively and realistic, with a water-filled carafe of flowers in which the window and other details of the room are excellently reflected, while the dew on the flowers is so exquisitely imitated that it seems real."

Another of the painter's biographers, Gian Pietro Bellori, saw the musician as a young girl, and certainly the ribbon in the hair is more feminine than masculine. But there are young pop musicians today who raise similar doubts.

The painting is so typical of Caravaggio that it is surprising to discover that the catalogue of his works lists no other musicians with the exception of one group in the Metropolitan Museum of Art in New York and the morose but beautiful figure in Munich. The lute player theme, however, accompanied the artist's influence and may be found in France in the works of Tournier and Valentin, and in the Netherlands in those of Honthorst, Bronchorst, Baburen, and Terbrugghen. Not that the theme was new. Angels have always played music, and artists have always liked the shapes of musical instruments. The novelty in this work lies not in its subject but in its light. Within this crystalline transparency, even the ray of sunshine that indicates the wall is merely a variation in color to brighten the background. Caravaggio's realism, as seen in the dew on the flower petals, the perfection of texture of the skin of the pears, the moist brilliance of the teeth and eyes, is of a pleasant kind, quite different from the squalor so dear to many seventeenth-century followers of the artist. His tragic accent has too often been confused with the effects they drew from poverty. Caravaggio was always up to the level of tragedy; his successors remained at that of melodrama. The musician here, whether boy or girl, has nothing in common with the little urchins scratching violins in the works of Antoine Le Nain. This smiling figure is composed without the slightest expressionistic indulgence and according to a very knowledgeable succession of forms, each rising from the other, all taking the form of the instrument, progressing from the hand to the shoulder, and thus diffusing in a wave the echoes of the shell where the music began. Beneath the charming surface lies complex geometry, which should not surprise those who recall the great symphonies of light and shadow that Caravaggio was to paint some years later in San Luigi dei Francesi in Rome.

GIAMBATTISTA TIEPOLO (Italian; 1696–1770)

Maecenas Presenting the Arts to Augustus

Painted about 1745

Oil on canvas, 27 1/4 × 35"

Catalogue No. 4.   Formerly Gatchina Palace

In addition to five immense paintings that belong to a cycle on Roman history of which three other panels are in the Metropolitan Museum of Art in New York and two in Vienna, the Hermitage owns three more paintings by Giambattista Tiepolo. This one was purchased from the artist in Venice around 1743–45 by Count Algarotti, agent for Frederick of Prussia and Augustus of Saxony. The allusion to the Emperor Augustus must have pleased the Saxon Elector. Dresden, however, did not keep all its Tiepolos. Some were sold at auction in Amsterdam in 1765, and it was then that the Hermitage acquired a huge *Cleopatra's Banquet* and a smaller painting on the same subject (these paintings were destined to travel, for the first was sold to the Melbourne Museum before the Second World War and the other went to the Musée Cognacq-Jay in Paris). This *Maecenas* also passed through Dresden, in the collection of Count von Brühl. Fortunately it has remained in Leningrad. In the work of Tiepolo, it stands between the *Transportation of the House of the Virgin from Nazareth to Loreto*, painted for the Church of the Scalzi in Venice, and the frescoes of the Labia Palace. That is to say, it is from the period when Tiepolo did not hesitate to place himself in the tradition of Veronese—it was perhaps his way of restraining himself and keeping his feet on the ground amidst the lavish decorations of columns and statues so dear to the Venetians. When he lifted his head toward the sky, it was to launch fantastic clouds that turned into angels, horses, or gods.

Tiepolo's reputation was international. Count Tessin wanted him to decorate the Royal Palace in Stockholm. Count von Greiffenklau invited him to Würzburg. Russia did not remain indifferent to his genius, and during the reign of Catherine II offered him a commission while he was still working in Madrid. For the Oranienbaum Palace, now renamed for Lomonosov, he painted a ceiling decoration on the theme of Mars and the Graces.

ANTONIO CANALETTO (Italian; 1697–1768)
Reception of a French Ambassador in Venice

Painted about 1740
Oil on canvas, 71 1/4 × 102 1/4"
Catalogue No. 175

The arrival of an ambassador was undoubtedly a much more spectacular event in the past than it is today; the arrival of an ambassador in Venice was always an entry into another world. Not only did it mean a journey into a unique setting, but also into an intellectual and spiritual climate that made the minister feel prouder to represent his country in the City of the Doges than anywhere else —even in the eighteenth century when Venice had lost much of her power and was no longer mistress of the seas. To enter Venice amidst all the pomp which the Serenissima knew how to display for its official receptions was to penetrate into the city of the *vedute*, those scenic views that all art lovers of the world wished to possess, and which had made Venetian landscapists so famous that they were invited to the four corners of Europe. It is understandable that the ambassadors themselves asked to be represented in these landscapes that were so highly prized by everyone.

Luca Carlevaris (1665–1731) depicted the arrival of the British ambassador in 1707 and again in 1726. In that same year Canaletto took up the theme for the arrival, on November 4, 1726, of the French ambassador. It seems, to judge from a comparable picture painted for the ambassador of the Holy Roman Empire in 1729, that the commission almost always included a companion piece representing an excursion of the Doge on board the state barge, the "Bucentaur." The companion piece to this painting of the French arrival is in the Pushkin Museum in Moscow.

It is remarkable that in all examples of this kind the important personage who commissioned the work, even if he were the Doge, did not mind being represented as very small in the picture, an outline a little more distinct than the others, barely separated from the crowd by a little respectful space, a somewhat larger boat, or a more visible costume. What was important was not so much to be one's self but to be in Venice. The city remained the prime subject of the picture. That in these representations, in which the hierarchy is not fixed by the pride of the ambassador nor by the brilliance of the nation he represented, it should be the city that prevails, and finally that, beyond the hundreds of figures and the city itself, one should recognize Canaletto—his manner of making the light flow through the clouds, of drenching the sky, of expressing here the sunlight, there the shadow, and the mist that turns Venice into a shimmering vision—is a miracle. In his ease in remaining himself while maneuvering so many elements, we see perhaps the culmination of the young artist's first experiments in designing sets for the operas of Vivaldi. To master such a theme as a Venetian popular festival, one would have had to be a stage designer.

FRANCESCO GUARDI (Italian; 1712–1793)
Venice

Undated
Oil on wood transferred to canvas, 10 5/8 × 9"
Catalogue No. 262

Francesco Guardi was one of the chroniclers of Venetian public ceremonies. He was also a land-scapist of the city and lagoon, and was especially skillful in evoking the city's melancholy atmosphere. Where Canaletto stressed animation, the lively movement of pedestrians in narrow streets, and the sharp, black brilliance of gondolas on the canals, Guardi painted deserted squares, and churches with outlines obscured by that unsettled fog that assures a prolonged vibration of color in space. There is, moreover, in Guardi a kind of dramatic sentiment when he paints crowds gathered for festive occasions or massed to watch the passage of the Doge. It is as if he wished to commemorate the city's precarious existence on the water, or to express the difficulties of the Venetian Republic, badly treated at the time by the great powers and even humiliated after centuries of splendor.

Guardi also painted "caprices"—scenes that cannot be recognized or identified—which are in their way imaginary echoes of Venice. In the same dampness, the same light that dissolves volume, he placed ruined palaces, the remains of majestic arches, broken obelisks, and eroded columns. It is as though the artist were evoking his city's future, a time when nothing will remain of its great homes and well-ordered squares except ruins among which the menders of nets will plant their awnings, and against which the sailors will lean their oars.

The landscape in the Hermitage lies on the borderline between pure invention and description. One might hesitate to say so, had the Venetians themselves not acknowledged it when the painting was shown at the Doges' Palace during the memorable 1965 exhibition that reconstructed the Guardi workshop. The scene is made up of elements borrowed here and there from the city. It is the quintessence of Venice, a distillation of that treeless city, beautiful as a stage set, on which pass the shadows of the actors in the greatest play of all—always to be seen in Venice—everyday life.

MASTER OF FLÉMALLE (Flemish; 1st half, 15th century)
Virgin and Child

Painted about 1435

Oil on wood, 13 1/2 × 9 1/2"

Catalogue No. 442.   Formerly Tatishchev Collection, willed to Nicholas I in 1845

It is sometimes difficult for scholars to establish the connection between unsigned works and the artists whose names are known from documents. A recent exhibition in Bruges of anonymous Primitives has shown the method used to reconstruct a personality. A painting that appears highly original is chosen, and around it are placed other works seemingly from the same brush. Small coherent groups are thus formed, to be taken as a whole or not at all, and which with luck may be enlarged. The method is not without its difficulties; this Madonna, for instance, was originally attributed to Rogier van der Weyden. Then it was found to be related to the *Mérode Altarpiece* (now in the Cloisters, Metropolitan Museum of Art, New York), which in turn showed a similarity to the *Nativity* of Dijon and the *Saint Barbara* in the Prado. This was enough to form the nucleus of a body of work by an original artist, provisionally christened the Master of Flémalle. Some believe that the Master could well have been Robert Campin, mentioned in documents as the teacher of Rogier van der Weyden, while partisans of Van der Weyden believe that Flémalle was simply their artist in his youth. If one day Campin's signature were to be found on a painting all this would be resolved, but this key is still missing, and all we can do is to make rather haphazard connections between the documents and the paintings.

Although the paintings attributed to the Master of Flémalle, including the Hermitage diptych, clearly antedate the full flowering of Rogier van der Weyden's talent, we must question whether they show only the first stages of a young artist's development. We note a very coherent view of the world, a manner of using perspective to say everything about people and objects. It is difficult to believe the artist would have discarded this with maturity. Geometry is here an instrument of inquiry; nothing remains uncertain. Everything is set down, from the water jug on the small table to the shadow of a blind on the wall and the dancing movement of the flames. Here there is a realism transcended by mysticism, which turns the scene of a mother warming her child by the fireplace into a work of meditation. The painter brings spiritual illumination into his own home, even showing the landscape outside as distorted by the thick glass panes of the window.

The left-hand panel of the diptych (number 433 in the catalogue), representing the Holy Trinity with the dead Christ lying across the knees of God and the Holy Spirit hovering above his shoulder, is an abrupt passage into another world, but the same calm reigns in both. Painted in similar colors, the two pictures were intended to be viewed side by side.

HUGO VAN DER GOES (Flemish; c. 1435–1482)
Lamentation over Christ
Undated
Oil on wood, 14 1/4 × 12"
Catalogue No. 4782

This work is a variant of one of the panels of a diptych in Vienna. Its origin is still obscure, but in any case the picture has a strength that belies its actual dimensions. A small panel monumental in concept, it is difficult to see it as the work of a contemporary of Memling or Dirk Bouts. What is crystalline and immobile in the works of those masters here gives way to an entirely different strength in which movement transcends the bodily forms, assembling them in a dramatic spirit reminiscent of the sixteenth century. Placing a dark gap—the Virgin's cloak—in the center of the painting is a theatrical device that allows the body of Christ to slip from all the pious arms trying to retain it. Death seems to draw it toward an abyss, from which we know that a great spiritual mystery will make it rise, so that its torment may be contemplated forever. Action surrounds this slipping movement: the Holy Women kiss the nails of the cross as though to obliterate the murder; the lovely Magdalene sits withdrawn in her solitude; the cross stands out against a stormy sky.

Other artists of the time, even the greatest Flemish tragic painters, handled the Descent from the Cross much more descriptively. This new vision of the Christian tragedy was probably conceived by the painter during his hours of solitude as a monk in the Red Cloister of Anderghem, in the Soignies Forest near Brussels. Even a trip to Italy would not explain his independent attitude toward Flemish painting of the period, for Van der Goes in his stark vision went far beyond Italian artists. His own contemporaries were aware of his truly original contribution. Gaspard Ofhuys wrote: "Thanks to his talent, the lay monk had gained the highest repute in our order; he was even more famous than if he had remained in the world." This is not customary praise.

In a manner perhaps less strained than the tighter Viennese version, the Hermitage painting offers a total expression of the tragic impact of the death of the righteous man upon his followers. The artist's mysticism, far from clothing the figures in rich or poor garments, restores them to the human condition without social classification. This fact gains interest when we recall that Hugo van der Goes, according to Robert Rey, was the first to paint Biblical shepherds like actual shepherds of his own time, with dirty hands in contrast to the white hands of rich merchants.

The Leningrad *Lamentation* is a great work, certainly not a copy, and as vibrant as the one in Vienna.

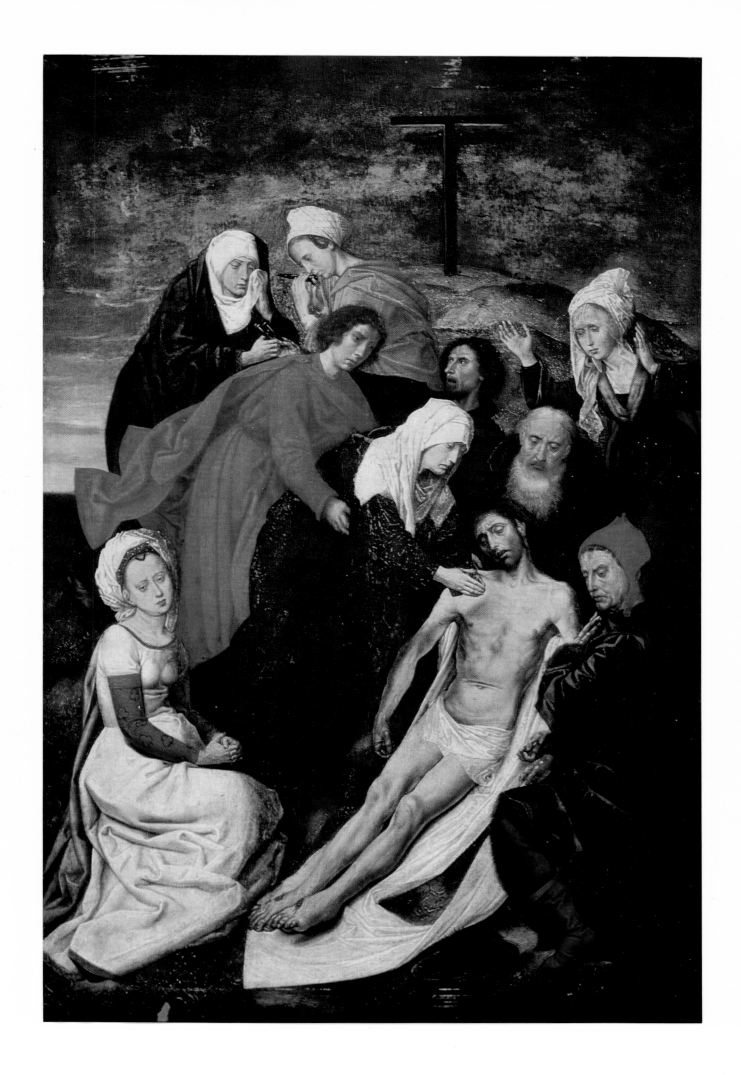

PETER PAUL RUBENS (Flemish; 1577–1640)
Perseus and Andromeda

Painted in 1612–21
Oil on wood transferred to canvas, 39 1/4 × 54 3/4"
Catalogue No. 461.   Formerly Brühl Collection

The dying monster lies stretched across the bottom of the painting, no longer dangerous, its sole purpose now being to provide an undulating line on which to construct a great pageant of whites, blues, yellows, golds, and reds—this is the liberation of Andromeda. Several times in his lifetime, Rubens enjoyed painting the marvelous encounter of a winged horse, an armor-clad warrior, and a beautiful naked girl on a rock; he makes it a splendid fête. This painting is usually compared to the Berlin version, which treats the same scene in reverse with the winged horse on the left and Andromeda on the right, and to a painting in the Prado, one of the master's last compositions, finished by Jordaens. The Berlin painting is less dense, more attentive to the situation within the decor of the scene, and to the positions and gestures of the figures. The relationships are clearer, and the story perhaps better told.

Here, instead, it seems to have been poured out in one breath. The painter has placed all the elements of the story together. The horse fills nearly half the canvas simply because Rubens enjoyed painting him. The other half is devoted to the contrast between the bronze, gold-trimmed armor of Perseus and the light, sometimes to the detriment of the soft swelling forms of the naked Andromeda. Cupids are everywhere, to link the protagonists and assure the continuity of the action. The painting turns around the serpent-haired head of Medusa in the center of the round shield, the single element of tragedy in a painting dedicated to the triumph of love, since Andromeda's ordeal ends with the arrival of Perseus. Rubens could paint tragic scenes, but for his mythological paintings he was first conscious of the physical joy of living. It would not be idle to compare this Andromeda, who steps radiantly from chains that seem scarcely cruel and which the cupids envelop in silken drapery, to the unhappy, shivering, chained Andromeda (The Hague) painted by Rembrandt during Rubens's lifetime—the reply of a troubled sensuality to this amorous exuberance. The division between Flemish Catholicism and Dutch Protestantism is not enough to explain the difference in treatment, which is one of temperament. Rembrandt did not depict the joys of the flesh until the end of his life.

PETER PAUL RUBENS (Flemish; 1577–1640)
Landscape with a Rainbow

Painted about 1632–35

Oil on wood transferred to canvas, 33 7/8 × 50 3/4"

Catalogue No. 482.   Formerly Brühl Collection

One is tempted at first to place Rubens's landscapes in the realm of fantasty. Day and night alternate in the same picture, and the painter pushes his horizons to the extreme limit of visibility. He gives us a feeling of the earth's roundness and does not hesitate to have medieval knights jousting in his valleys, as if he were a true Romantic. Yet his countless sketches of trees, hills, and farms prove that he studies nature with the avidity of an impassioned realist.

Rubens adopted all the aspects of landscape painting found in his predecessors. He knows the infinite blue of Bruegel's horizons; he makes use of Dürer's sense of a fragmented world; he does not neglect Altdorfer's system of painting leaves; and he even approaches the strange scenic effects so dear to Cranach. However, Rubens eludes classification because he took what he wanted without restriction—dancers, lovers, sheep, mountains, a bridge, a rainbow—and used them all effortlessly, as he did the styles of other artists. After all, he was accustomed to painting gods, kings, and Venus herself.

Sometimes his composition is so obvious that it seems simple. This work, however, is distinctly complex. The entire landscape balances in a movement that ripples into the double arches of the bridge and up into the great arc in the sky, almost directly in the center of the work. The foreground offers an elementary demonstration of the genius of Rubens, as disparate masses of men and beasts interpenetrate to form the base of the painting. Its rhythm establishes a force which is increased by the luminous accents, while a vertical light fades toward the right and dissolves, having returned the painting to its center, the bridge. This rich, deliberate structure gives rise to a picture of exceptional density. We might compare it to another and very similar version in the museum of Valenciennes, in which the eye is guided in a more pronounced way by a flock of sheep dispersing in the meadow. In the Hermitage picture, Rubens's rhetoric is more elliptical; the delicacy of conception increases one's sensitivity to nature. The painter allows no confusion to appear—everything is assured and familiar, and love revolves like the solar system. Nothing is obscure, all is fresh and marvelous. After more than three centuries, this painting supplies a lesson in optimism. We see that the painter needed many elements to express his happiness, and that Rubens only came into his own when he stood at the summit of a mountain of images and ideas. This may be surprising nowadays when people see the whole universe in the outline of a pebble.

ANTHONY VAN DYCK (Flemish; 1599–1641)
Portrait of a Man

Painted about 1620

Oil on canvas, 49 1/8 × 33 3/4"

Catalogue No. 552.   Formerly Crozat Collection

The Hermitage owns twenty-six paintings by Van Dyck, principally from the Walpole and Crozat collections. This ensemble is equaled only by the collections of the British Crown and may even surpass them in diversity. This portrait is dated approximately 1620 but is not really a work of the artist's youth, for the astonishingly precocious Van Dyck studied with a master when he was only ten and, by the age of fourteen, painted entirely acceptable portraits. Rubens, of course, hastened to invite the young man to join his workshop, although there is nothing to prove that he made him his right-hand assistant. The records reveal Van Dyck's independence of character, and it seems less and less probable that he let himself be dominated by Rubens, although this does not mean that he entirely escaped Rubens's influence.

This portrait, if it dates from the years before Van Dyck's journey to Italy, represents a happy moment in the history of the seventeenth-century portrait. Few paintings by other artists of the time are so simple or so free, while its liveliness is rare even for Van Dyck. Ordinarily he strove to express the power, nobility, or charm of his models, but here it is the intelligence that he conveys. One imagines that the artist, an intellectual prodigy, responded to a personality willing to accept such a spontaneous, scarcely posed, and unpretentious representation of himself. It is as though he were caught in a moment of discussion, and the work could pass as a detail from a larger composition depicting some debate such as Rubens suggests in his *Four Philosophers* (Florence, Pitti Palace) or Titian in his *Pope Paul III and His Nephews* (Naples). Comparisons are dangerous, but is it not Van Dyck who shows more naturalness and ease?

According to tradition, this man was an Antwerp physician, later distinguished by being called with a colleague to the bedside of the dying Rubens in 1640. The archives mention the "care administered by Lazarus and Spinola to the patient's feet." The enlightened conversationalist in Van Dyck's portrait is probably Dr. Lazarus.

LUCAS VAN LEYDEN (Dutch; 1489/94–1533)
Healing of the Blind Man of Jericho
Painted about 1531
Oil on wood transferred to canvas, 45 1/4 × 59 1/4"
Catalogue No. 407.   Formerly Crozat Collection

"Of all the works of Lucas van Leyden," wrote the Dutch painter and historian Karel van Mander in 1602, "the finest is a cabinet with two doors at present owned by Hendrick Goltzius, the eminent Haarlem artist, who for a large sum and to his great delight bought it in Leyden in 1602, his vast knowledge of art having given him a warm admiration for the works of Lucas. The subject represented is 'the blind man of Jericho,' Bartimeus, son of Timeus, restored to sight." Van Mander then quotes a poem that ends as follows:

From the light itself, the blind man had the light,
And Lucas, by that blind man, renders sight
To the blind brush of painters to whom he shows the way.

This old description is extremely valuable first of all for its authentication of the hand of Lucas in the Hermitage painting. A great many pictures attributed to this artist are merely painted transcriptions of his graphic works done by other men. In addition, Van Mander's admiration sums up that of the sixteenth-century Mannerists who found in Lucas van Leyden the precursor of their own lively rhythms, gaudy colors, and whimsicality in perspective as well as costuming.

If we retain 1494 as the most probable date of Lucas van Leyden's birth, he was extremely precocious, being not yet fifteen when he engraved the masterpiece *Mohammed and the Monk*. His interests were varied, for he treated religious and Biblical themes and introduced the genre painting that was to become the pride of the Dutch. He outshone his contemporaries Gossaert, Scorel, and Mostaert, and under the pressure of new ideas, was among the artists who most forcefully disturbed the old traditions of painting retables. And yet he always remained essentially a graphic artist even in his paintings, where he showed himself to be more a "colorer" than a painter. In him we see the whole expression of the crisis that overtook Northern art when it received the shock of the Renaissance, a shock whose effects it is exciting to follow in the works of Dürer, Cranach, and Metsys, all of them, like Lucas, troubled by the new freedom and trying to adapt it to their native tendencies and profound beliefs. This was perhaps more difficult in art than in philosophy. Erasmus was easily the peer of the greatest Italian thinkers. But we can measure all the difficulties of Lucas van Leyden by recalling that he was the almost exact contemporary of Correggio (1494–1534).

FRANS HALS (Dutch; c. 1581–1666)
Portrait of a Man
Painted about 1650–60
Oil on canvas, 33 1/4 × 26 1/2"
Catalogue No. 816.   Acquired between 1763 and 1774

Opinions differ on the date of this painting, one of the great male portraits in the career of Frans Hals. The Hermitage catalogue places it about 1660, during the period of the *Portrait of a Man* in The Hague, the *Man Wearing a Hat* in Kassel, and the close version of the latter in Cambridge. The reasons for this opinion are easy to follow. This painting shows something of the dazzling brushwork characteristic of the last portraits. To be sure, paint, for Hals, was never simply color placed on a surface, but his immediate language. Nevertheless, as he approached the age of eighty, his strokes became looser and broader; no longer are there only a few vibrant accents, but the whole painting begins to billow in great surging movements. Indeed, such movements are found here in the loose folds of the black garment. This portrait of a slightly exasperated man with an inquisitorial look, whose hat is now hidden under several overpaintings, is therefore conceivably related to the pictures mentioned above; it would not even be far removed from the man who seems about to fall into a drunken sleep in the midst of the group of Regents of the Haarlem Almshouse. A further parallel may be noted in the manner of suggesting a cuff in the foreground by means of a few strokes of white.

Another opinion is that of the organizers of the Hals retrospective exhibition held in Haarlem in 1962. The Hermitage had lent this painting, while the Museum of Odessa had sent two figures of saints, works of the artist's youth. The Dutch catalogue notes the stylistic freedom, but finds that the treatment of face and hair does not show equal facility. As a result, it places the work in the years 1650–52.

Could not the disparity between the free treatment of the clothing and the restraint of the face be explained by the fact that this was a commissioned portrait and that Hals was forced to moderate his style? Rembrandt, at the end of his life, did the same, painting in two manners, one for figures, the other for portraits, and neither manner was exempt from traces of the other.

The Hermitage owns another Hals portrait, the *Man with a Glove*, and one of the rare works of his son, Frans Hals the Younger, entitled the *Young Soldier*.

REMBRANDT (Dutch; 1606–1669)
Flora

Painted in 1634
Oil on canvas, 47 1/2 × 39 3/4"
Catalogue No. 732.   Formerly Arentz Collection

There are many ways of looking at this picture. First, as a figure of fantasy—it was sold under the title *Lady Dressed as a Shepherdess* in Amsterdam in 1770. Later it was called the *Jewish Fiancée*, although the *Jewish Encyclopedia* has never recognized anything Jewish in the various Rembrandt paintings to which this adjective has been applied. Another interpretation turned to Rembrandt's family and suggested that the work was a portrait of Saskia, the young woman whom the artist married on July 10, 1634. There is another, more stately version of the flower-decked woman—the canvas of about the same size, dated traditionally 1635, in the National Gallery, London. There she is called *Saskia van Ulenborch in Arcadian Costume*, that is to say, a mythological shepherdess. This does not prevent some critics from calling her Proserpine, kidnapped while gathering flowers by her uncle Pluto to become Queen of the Underworld.

The Russians still call her Flora, goddess of flowers and gardens, while emphasizing that this is a portrait of Saskia. Some critics argue that if she were a goddess she would carry a cornucopia and not a leafy, flowered staff. Others find the staff an allusion to the courtesan Flora, and thus Saskia becomes the patroness of prostitutes. One could explore mythological dictionaries *ad infinitum*.

That Rembrandt leaves the experts so divided should make us simply admit that he wished to paint his young wife in one of the theatrical costumes he liked to put on his models, and that, being concerned with representing a goddess, he thought principally of describing Saskia as he imagined her. If he needed this costuming to put her in the realm of the fantastic, it was not the realm codified by mythologists.

Beneath its disguise the portrait is very strange. It is, at first glance, a young woman crowned with flowers and carrying a flowered scepter. However, as is often true in Rembrandt, the major image is accompanied by secondary, sometimes contradictory, images that heighten the meaning and give it greater resonance. A kind of deep gaping mouth seems to open near the fresh young figure. Is it perhaps an ordinary vine-covered rock or a stone animal overgrown with moss, the kind of ornament found in old gardens? In any case, it is a troubling presence, confirmed by a certain effect of animal eyes shining in the embroideries of the dress. Psychoanalysts would perhaps find a hint of sexuality and its mysteries. The painting is traditionally compared to a later portrait of Hendrickje, Rembrandt's mistress, in a pose suggesting the Flora theme. Saskia holds her place in the artist's complex universe as well as she can, but Hendrickje will be presented more simply, a young woman who returns carrying flowers in her apron (Metropolitan Museum of Art, New York). Then, Rembrandt no longer needs mystery and symbols—reality charms him enough.

REMBRANDT (Dutch; 1606–1669)
Danaë

Painted in 1636
Oil on canvas, 73 × 79"
Catalogue No. 723.   Formerly Crozat Collection

This painting is not only beautiful, it attests to a metamorphosis of the artist. Previously, the feminine presence in Rembrandt's work was uneasy and disturbed. It manifested itself in the kidnapping of a terrorized Proserpine, or in an Andromeda bound sadistically in chains while she waited for the handsome knight on the winged horse. The sexuality in these works is accompanied by well-known Freudian images—a stallion running wild, the snarling muzzles of wild beasts. Then Rembrandt suddenly discarded this panicky mobilization of the human being and his myths in the face of sex, and painted this picture. It is impossible to look at it without thinking of the simplicity that his nudes will acquire much later, when he is in his sixties—a time difficult to take for old age —when he will finally draw, paint, or engrave the female nude with desire but without problems. Here the approach to the woman, although demythologized, is still not entirely direct. If one calls these deviations eroticism, then the *Danaë* is an erotic painting, full of recesses and amorous hollows, a painting openly waiting for someone who may be the spectator but is more likely the great golden pillar that upholds the bed curtains. The work teems with repetitions, double meanings, ambiguous ideas that all contribute to the same purpose: a preparation for lovemaking. The *Danaë* is undoubtedly the happy result of Rembrandt's marriage. However, the face is not that of Saskia and bears a strong resemblance to that of an unknown woman whose portrait, dated 1635, is now in the Cleveland Museum of Art.

But even if we know nothing of the person represented here, we are still fascinated by a certain persistence of themes maintained by the painter in confronting the women in his life. There are the parallel paintings of Saskia as Flora and a flower-decked Hendrickje. There is also a reprise of this *Danaë*, a woman half-rising from bed, fairly easy to recognize as Hendrickje, although some historians think she is Geertje Dircx, nurse to Titus about 1642. That work, dating from the late 1640s, is in Edinburgh and has been called *Sarah Waiting for Tobias on Their Wedding Night*, a title that could be applied to our *Danaë*, since there is no shower of gold. If Rembrandt really had this theme in mind (the Edinburgh catalogue calls the painting simply *Woman in Bed*) it is interesting to note that Sarah had considerable difficulty in losing her virginity. The demon had killed seven successive husbands, and the Angel Raphael had to intervene so that Tobias might escape the monster and spend the night in grateful prayer with his young bride. This apocryphal legend may serve to remind us that Rembrandt had to overcome many taboos before he could admit the pleasures of the flesh. The simplicity of the Edinburgh painting contrasts strongly with the extreme ingenuity, the elaborate staging that here reveal a nude woman hidden in an amorous ambiance.

REMBRANDT (Dutch; 1606–1669)
Holy Family
Painted in 1645
Oil on canvas, 46 1/8×35 7/8"
Catalogue No. 741.   Formerly Crozat Collection

The Holy Family in a Dutch period interior was not a new idea for Rembrandt in 1645. A similar scene, dated about 1633, showing the carpenter's tools in the background shadows, hangs in the museum in Munich. The work is simply a family portrait: father, mother, and child, together with the cradle, form a homogeneous block, and there is nothing to indicate holiness except the discreet allusion in the artisan's tools. Twelve years later, Rembrandt, having experienced the tumult of the Baroque, knows the value of gestures, the pathos of movement, and the effect of angelic intervention, as he has shown in the *Sacrifice of Abraham*. He is approaching the moment when he will give his compositions more unity, when he will arrange everything freely within the painting. More than ever, the picture will become an entity from which no detail can be detached.

The composition of the *Holy Family* is a complex arrangement, with three figures at once together and separated from each other. The child sleeps. The mother reads and bends over him without closing her book. The father wields his ax, making something that may be the handle of a scythe. A fire burns on the hearth. From the base of the cradle to the top of the handle these elements are locked in a triangle which quietly suggests unity and intimacy. Nobody inside the triangle is aware of the flight of winged children descending into the room, although the leading cherub, wings open, plummets down toward the cradle like a tiny celestial parachutist.

The Musée Léon Bonnat in Bayonne owns a drawing that is undoubtedly the first idea for this painting. It is drawn with a few quick strokes of the pen. The fireplace is there; the cradle, the Virgin, and Joseph are already set down as a unity on which varying intensities of light will later indicate the degrees of importance. And the flight of the angel is shown in the upper left. But everything in the sketch is airier and more nervous than in the painting, where the color and forms lend their weight to provide the contrast that sets off the wonder of the miracle so well—the calm of a simple family scene.

REMBRANDT (Dutch; 1606–1669)

Return of the Prodigal Son

Painted about 1668–69

Oil on canvas, 103 1/8 × 80 3/4"

Catalogue No. 742.   Formerly Archbishop Clement Augustus Collection, Cologne

This huge panel clearly belongs to Rembrandt's last years. The painting is no longer spread out as before, but truly built up, as we also see in such late works as the *Conspiracy of Julius Civilis* (Stockholm) of 1662, the last *Self-Portrait*, 1669 (Cologne), the *Family Portrait* (Brunswick), or the *Jewish Bride* (Amsterdam). Some consider Rembrandt's last works superior in quality and personality to all his others. This is an entirely justifiable opinion, with, however, a suggestion of modernism about it—the kind of modernism that expects an artist to do less than his best work when he is assigned a public or private commission. People are more attracted to the lonely Rembrandt, the artist neglected by his own city and by his collectors, the unhappy man who had lost his faithful companion and his only son, the free Rembrandt, painting as he had never painted before, surpassing himself when people misunderstood and rejected his art. The image of an old man rising above indifference and disdain by the sheer power of his genius is a captivating one. Its fault lies in its dependence on an excessive isolation of works whose special quality lies in their having developed, rapidly but without a break, from what went before.

The slower, easier rhythm so admired in this painting—almost a return to the early Primitive manner of lining up figures side by side—had been heralded for almost twenty years. It begins when Rembrandt adopts the conception of a painting as a continuous texture more than as a theatrical setting; that is to say, when he goes beyond great compositional effects to become more of a painter, when he enters entirely into the movements of his brush.

The evolution of this tendency induced a gradual heightening of color. While the aging Frans Hals locked himself into a counterpoint of white and black, Rembrandt permitted himself intensities of color that are still so striking that we may easily imagine their strength when he laid them on his canvases. He went over completely to the radiant force of color, moving perhaps further than ever from his Baroque compositions and from narrative. In this *Return of the Prodigal Son*, a boy kneels and some standing figures watch him. When we compare this simplicity with the elaborate complexity of a drawing on the same subject done twenty years before (Teylers Museum, Haarlem) we see how much Rembrandt changed, how he detached himself from his earlier principles of animation. Nevertheless, the artist who painted the *Sacrifice of Abraham* and the artist who painted this work are two aspects of the same man, the first grandiloquent, the second meditative. Rembrandt can only be grasped in his entirety through the works produced during his entire lifetime.

GERARD TER BORCH (Dutch; 1617–1681)

The Glass of Lemonade

Undated

Oil on wood transferred to canvas, 26 3/8 × 21 1/4"

Catalogue No. 881.   Formerly Malmaison Collection of the Empress Josephine

Unlike the noisy interiors of Jan Steen, so full of the sound of breaking crockery, Ter Borch offers silence. The action is accomplished in small, restrained gestures. The setting is not an inventory of objects, of which there are only a few. If there are pictures hanging on the walls, we know still less than in other painters what they represent; the gleam of the gold frame is enough. His women live in reasonable, middle-class Dutch comfort, have few servants, and are generally warmly wrapped up against the chill of their inadequately heated homes. Sometimes, Ter Borch recounts a slight anecdote, but the story never controls the painting and may even be disregarded. In his Louvre painting, a soldier offers money to a woman, and what in other painters would immediately prompt the title *Brothel Scene* suggests nothing more than *The Gallant Officer*. In this Hermitage painting, the outline of the bed in the background, the coercing hand of the old woman, the young woman's reticence toward the elegant young man who has not removed his hat, but grasps the girl's hand on the flimsy pretext of a glass of lemonade, might very well suggest calling the picture *The Procuress*.

But this is a Ter Borch and we remain in the realm of good taste. This is assured for once and for all by the majority of his other interior scenes dominated by pleasant young women busily making music, or writing or receiving letters, for the Low Countries too had their literary circles and their bluestockings. What we know of Ter Borch's family suggests that he himself lived in the cultured bourgeois society of his time.

If it is sometimes difficult to see the witty and satiric aspects of his works, it is because of the quality of the painting itself—transparent as porcelain, lustrous as silver, quivering like tulle and, under the light, vibrant as silk. Lovers of "finish" went wild at the time over the illusion of fabric in some paintings by Meiris. The painting of Ter Borch, equally faithful, goes beyond illusion. One of his most characteristic works is in the Dresden Museum—a painting, a stool, a bed hidden behind tentlike draperies, all brought to life by a young woman seen from the back in a satin gown, her neck of a pearly whiteness and her golden hair plaited. There is another Ter Borch in the Hermitage, hanging near our painting, in which the same magic—of a woman seen from the back—operates. Only in Vermeer is reality so peaceful. By comparison, this little meeting may seem quite talkative. But look closely: there is really nothing but a glass of lemonade and two young people looking at each other.

ADAM PYNACKER (Dutch; 1622–1673)
Boat on a River
Painted about 1655
Oil on canvas, 17 1/4 × 14 5/8"
Catalogue No. 1093.   Formerly Crozat Collection

The Italians have always been rather uneasy about the kind of Italian landscape that was not their own discovery but that of foreign artists. But it is not surprising that this everyday reality should have been revealed by visitors rather than by the native inhabitants, obliged to transform their usual environment in order to see it. It is thus to Van Vittel that we owe the birth of Venetian landscape painting which rose to such prodigious heights in the eighteenth century. Italian landscapists soon moved along well-defined paths, leaving the foreign artists to persist in painting what their native public expected from their stay in Italy.

Adam Pynacker is one of those Dutch landscapists, like Berchem, Breenberg, Karel Dujardin, De Moucheron, and Cornelis van Poelenburgh, who crossed the Alps in search of the traditional aesthetic lesson and discovered a quite different precept—that of exoticism. The Alpine drawings of Bruegel and Roelandt Savery remind us of the fascination of sun and mountains for painters from the North. However, the artists overcame their astonishment at hills where the sun sinks behind cork oaks, or at the sight of Virgilian herds of goats crossing dry riverbeds in summer. They often chose themes in which, consciously or not, they recognized something of their native land, some glimpse of the Dutch world of landlocked waters (the open sea is rarely found in Dutch painting), just as Van Gogh was to love the drawbridges of Provence because they are so common in Holland. Possibly, the lagoon silence of this painting accounts for its having been taken for a Dutch landscape of Adriaen van de Velde, although everything in it speaks of Italy: the architecture on the shore, the casks on the boat, and the sky—bluer than is allowed in the village near Delft where its actual creator, Adam Pynacker, was born.

During the exhibition of Dutch landscapists who worked in Italy, held in Utrecht in 1965, the compilers of the catalogue suggested some time around 1655 as the probable date of this painting. The work is characteristic of Pynacker's broken style, his manner of building up a painting in a succession of planes, surfaces, and rhythms foreign to the commonplace subject. Pynacker may have gone to Italy to find a crystal in which reality is shattered so as to assert itself more strongly in its pictorial resurrection.

JAN STEEN (Dutch; 1626–1679)
The Drinkers

Undated

Oil on wood, 15 3/8 × 11 3/4"

Catalogue No. 875.   Purchased in Berlin, 1764

It is generally believed that the work of Jan Steen can be summed up by a few trivial works which, along with those of Adriaen van Ostade, Brouwer, and even Frans Hals, are the equivalents, in the small dimensions for the Dutch home, of the large panels of popular festivals by Jordaens. Certainly there was a ready public in the towns that enjoyed these satires on rustic life, products of the Bruegelian tradition. And indeed there still is; the tramp holds his place in so-called humorous drawings.

Genre painting is a precious source of information on the customs of the period, and historians attentively examine its least detail. For example, there was the surprise of discovering, among the pictures represented in an interior by Jan Steen, a reduced replica of a painting of Frans Hals. One result has been that much attention has been paid to the elements of Steen's work and little to the painter himself.

In reality, his career was very diverse. In certain ways he is connected with the Mannerists, and in others is not so far removed from the subtleties of Dou and Meiris. He painted some figures in the tranquil atmosphere cultivated by Pieter de Hooch and Ochtervelt, in the circle of Vermeer. Finally, in his Biblical scenes, he showed himself susceptible to a certain rhetorical theatricality similar to Rembrandt's early Baroque works. Throughout all these experiments, which may correspond to his travels (born in Leyden, he lived in The Hague, kept a beer tavern in Delft, settled in Haarlem, and finally returned to Leyden), he succeeds in maintaining a personal style that shows in his lively accents and nervous line.

For this painting, Steen is said to have posed himself and his wife, Marghareta, daughter of the landscapist Van Goyen. The subject is the ravages of tobacco, against which Dutch pastors thundered in vain from their pulpits. It is unlikely, however, that Steen had taken up the cudgels of the moralists. He was always amused by the human comedy just as Molière enjoyed the clumsiness and trickery of peasants. Steen was to spread his good humor over the whole society of his time, from the farms to the homes of burgomasters. It is amusing to think that while here he has disguised himself and his wife as peasants, in the family portrait in the collection of the Nelson-Atkins Gallery in Kansas City the couple are dressed in their best. He is conversing with his father-in-law; she, in her silk finery, is playing on a spinet supported by sculptured cherubs, in a magnificent setting full of precious marbles, while a small Negro servant puts some wine to cool. Everything was a game in the work of Jan Steen.

PIETER DE HOOCH (Dutch; 1629–c. 1684)
Lady with Her Servant
Painted about 1660
Oil on canvas, 20 7/8 × 16 1/2"
Catalogue No. 943

This picture belongs to the period when the painter lived in Delft, between the ages of thirty and forty, the period thought to be the best in his career. In fact, we ordinarily prefer the Dutch in the simplicity of the first years of their republic, before they began to wear wigs and beribboned costumes, to have their portraits painted in front of columns, and to forget the soft light of the small bubble-glass panes through which it is so pleasant to watch boats passing on the canal. Thus, people favor the works that Pieter de Hooch painted in Delft. One day, perhaps, the last and worldly period of this painter will be rehabilitated. This is even probable, for in the history of art no tendency is condemned and everything is analyzed with the same curiosity, possibly for want of any real passion. Before this happens, however, we will have to escape a little from the fascination of Vermeer, the silence of his figures who fit so perfectly into the setting and are as mute as the tiled floors and the shutters. Pieter de Hooch painted some pictures in this spirit, as did Emmanuel de Witte and Ochtervelt; there were a few artists who participated in the search for this crystalline moment in painting, but only Vermeer persevered and made of it an *oeuvre*.

Hints of the elegance and sharp line revealed in the second part of De Hooch's career may be seen in his earliest works. The three paintings by him that hang side by side in the Hermitage sum up the artist's diverse qualities. *The Concert*, a late work, is broadly painted and is primarily a study of the shimmer of light and shade on volumes; there are even some of those motes of light so admired in Vermeer, curiously maintained in a period said to represent a decline. The *Lady with Her Servant*, an earlier work, insists more on a rather sharp definition of forms. The third, *The Soldier and the Servant*, combines the qualities of light and line of the other two. This ensemble, in three stages, traces the work of an artist of great sensibility, who, using the most common and hackneyed formulas of Dutch genre painting, succeeded in revealing his own originality and making his own voice heard.

This painting also shows how close Pieter de Hooch remained to the Primitives. His representation of a world partitioned by little walls, the minuteness of detail extending into the most distant perspective planes, is clearly the result of an artistic development inspired by the retable scenes of the Master of Alkmaar and Geertgen tot Sint Jans of Leyden.

JACOB VAN RUISDAEL (Dutch; 1628/29–1682)
The Morass

Painted about 1665

Oil on canvas, 28 1/2 × 39"

Catalogue No. 934

Jacob van Ruisdael's father, Isaac, was a frame-maker in Haarlem, who is thought to have taught his son the elements of drawing. The artist was undoubtedly trained by his uncle, Salomon van Ruisdael (1600/2–1670), and may have worked for a while with a cousin of his own age who was also a painter. This was a whole family of landscapists, but no group, no matter how tightly knit, is immune to outside impulses, and in the early works of Jacob van Ruisdael we find the influence of another Haarlem painter, Cornelis Vroom.

But none of his relatives or teachers ever went to the heart of Dutch landscape like this artist, about whose life we know little. We know that at the age of forty-eight he received a diploma in medicine from the University of Caen in France, and that he registered himself as a physician in Amsterdam; but we would be wrong to interpret this as a sign of amateurism. Ruisdael treated landscape both in the distance and up close; he depicted castles, towns, canals, and mills in such a way that we recognize Kostverloren Manor, Haarlem, the Zuiderzee near Muiden, the Wijk Mill, and thus he contributed to that vast inventory of national landscape that today enables us, through countless works of countless artists, to recapture the look of seventeenth-century Holland. He did this with feeling, as a personal choice in which he believed, and his representation of celebrated monuments did not prevent him from achieving a personal expression as strong as the landscapes of Rembrandt. His painting of the famous Jewish cemetery of Oudekerk, now in the museum in Dresden, is a meditation on a place truly inhabited by supernatural presences.

He was also the painter of a clump of trees at the top of a sand embankment, of a sprinkling of light snow on a meadow, of a few blighted flowers on a windy dune—all things that the French seventeenth century, afraid of the natural world, of untrimmed, untidy nature, and the trackless wilderness, carefully avoided.

In this painting of a forest pool, Ruisdael may have wished simply to return to the source lost to city dwellers, but his tragic gift led him far beyond a simple evocation of natural reality. The quiet water and the majestic sky contrast with the trunks of fallen trees or those ready to fall. A little peace lingers in the shade of these huge cadavers, near which the trunks of those still living writhe in painful torment. One cannot look at such a painting without slipping into a kind of anthropomorphism, without seeing there the expression of old human obsessions: how can we live so close to decomposition? What strange reciprocity exists between the two states we believe to be so well separated, life and death? The forest pool is more than a landscape: it is a crucible for meditation.

LUCAS CRANACH THE ELDER (German; 1472–1553)

Portrait of a Woman

Painted in 1526

Oil on wood, 35 × 23"

Catalogue No. 683

Compared to the tragic intensity of Grünewald, the fine sense of order wrested from existence with such difficulty by Dürer, and the sublime humanity of Holbein, Lucas Cranach the Elder, court painter, master of a flourishing workshop, and active partisan of the Reformation, offers an *oeuvre* less easily reduced to a few principles than that of his most famous contemporaries. Historians must take account of it under numerous headings.

This painting belongs to the genre perhaps least esteemed in the artist's career, for it comes under the heading devoted to the "court painter of Wittenberg." The date, 1526, at one time led to the belief that this was a portrait of pretty Sibylla von Cleve who, that year, at the age of fourteen, married Johann Friedrich of Saxony. Cranach's portrait of her in her bridal dress still hangs in the Weimar Museum, and paintings and prints from his workshop had circulated her image in all the neighboring courts. Then, in 1900, the German critic Flechsig withdrew the painting from the list of Lucas Cranach the Elder's works and attributed it to his eldest son, Hans, an artist about whom little is known and to whom many uncertain works are assigned. At the Hermitage, however, the charming work still bears the attribution to Cranach the Elder.

It is still difficult to see it as a portrait, for it is rather one of those images of beauty that is called Salome or Lucretia when shown with a sword, Cleopatra when with an asp, or Venus when disrobed. Heiresses of the mystery seen in the faces of Botticelli, and the smile that Leonardo da Vinci gave to the *Mona Lisa*, they are illustrations of the eternal feminine that Cranach loved: almond-eyed, hair pleasingly curled, the slim body wearing an elaborate dress like a second skin, plump hands with no other purpose than to wear rings and bestow caresses. Cranach's draftsmanship becomes sharp when he paints them; he digs into the panel as if he were engraving; each curve has the charm of the line of a supple body.

Scholars find this exquisite sensuality less pleasing than the bloody crucifixions, the exceptionally lively and comprehensive portraits, or some of the mythological scenes. But when we are confronted by one of these little sphinxes, too overdressed not to be delightful hussies, we say without hesitation: "Cranach." And we are much more certain than before his portraits of Martin Luther or his Madonnas.

296.

EL GRECO (Spanish; 1541–1614)
Saint Peter and Saint Paul

Painted about 1590

Oil on canvas, 47 1/4 × 41 1/4"

Catalogue No. 390.   Gift of P. P. Dournovo, 1911

In El Greco the sky is open. The wind that blows on his figures and swells their robes is not an earthly one, but comes from the spirit. The vault of heaven cracks under a thrust from the Beyond. When the hour of truth finally strikes, and the earthly images of saintliness must all be refashioned, those of El Greco will remain unchanged, since they have already passed beyond the physical into the metaphysical world. One recalls a remark by the painter Zuloaga, quoted by Marañón. Zuloaga said that just as there was *"cante jondo,"* or song that came from the depths, so many of El Greco's works were *"pintura jonda."* And, indeed, is there not something of the cry that rises from the depths of man's soul to be found in his pictures?

In this double image of the two apostles, the cry is again uttered in the tradition of exalted language. The work is stable, supported by a heightening of clear color as by a pillar of faith, while the faces are truly those of the just who have already experienced the Last Judgment. Peter's sweetness is born of grave doubts and great suffering. By contrast, Paul gives the impression of wearing armor beneath the garment that envelops him like a flame. Fist on the book, he is the man with no doubts, one who knows, a knight fighting for a righteous cause.

El Greco painted a great number of apostles and saints for the countless churches of Toledo, the holy city. There are, for example, 128 variations on the theme of Saint Francis.

Until quite recently, scholars were disturbed by what they read as the date 1614 under the signature monogram on this painting, since they refused to concede that the painter had constructed this work, solid as a rock, during the period of his most emotional vision of the Apocalypse. Now that the date has been deciphered to mean "made by" in the Greek characters with which the artist always signed his works, it is easier to place the painting a few years after the *Burial of Count Orgaz* (1586).

FRANCISCO DE ZURBARÁN (Spanish; 1598–1664)

The Virgin Mary as a Child

Painted about 1650

Oil on canvas, 29 × 21"

Catalogue No. 306.   Formerly Coesvelt Collection

Zurbarán painted three variations on the theme of the very young girl rapt in divine contemplation. The earliest work, now in the Collegiate Church in Jerez, was painted before 1630; the second is in the Metropolitan Museum of Art in New York; the last, painted about 1650, is in the Hermitage. The historian Paul Guimard has compared the three works, which supply in themselves a general summary of the artist's development.

The Jerez painting has some of the qualities of a snapshot. The child rests her elbow on a chair; eyes closed, she turns her face to a soothing light whose effect contrasts pleasingly with the almost geometric modeling of her robe. The New York painting suggests a theatrical stage. The Virgin sits between draperies, lifting her wet eyes toward heaven while a garland of cherubs forms a halo around her head. Every object in the painting seems suspended in space—a basket, a book, a pair of embroidery scissors, a bouquet of lilies—the whole setting escapes the rhythm of the earth and belongs, like the child, to the weightless state of the celestial world. The work is a fine example of the manner in which Zurbarán pushed realism to its extreme of purity. Under his brush, reality becomes a mystic presence, and the folds of the curtain belong more to the realm of the imagination than to the study from life.

The Hermitage painting is the work of an artist who has learned simplicity with age, and no longer needs geometric effects, the excesses of realism, or the display of grief. With the utmost discretion, he paints a seated child, hands folded on her forgotten embroidery, tearless, and without lilies or book or swaying curtains. And if, in this discretion, we still recognize the hand and mind of the artist, is that not proof that he has triumphed, and that in going beyond his most cherished formulas and trying to paint like everyone else, he painted as he alone knew how?

DIEGO VELÁZQUEZ (Spanish; 1599–1660)
Three Men at Table

Painted in 1617
Oil on canvas, 42 1/8 × 39 3/4"
Catalogue No. 389. Formerly Coesvelt Collection

This luncheon scene was painted before the artist reached his majority, while he was still assistant to the painter Pacheco in Seville, and hence only seven or eight years after the death of Caravaggio, whose *Supper at Emmaus* was perhaps its source. In considering the formation of Velázquez, the artist, we must take into account the pictorial vigor of his first teacher, Herrera the Elder, the still lifes of Cotán, and perhaps, because war brings people together as much as it divides them, the Dutch painters of Utrecht, all followers of Caravaggio in their fashion. We must not forget Jordaens, whose *Satyr and Peasant* foreshadows the *Drunkards Surrounding Bacchus* that Velázquez will paint about 1628, the crowning achievement of his period of "popular" subjects.

This painting, along with its variations and copies in the Budapest Museum and three private collections (Madrid, Zurich, Paris), is one of a group that includes the *Old Cook* (Edinburgh), the *Water-Carrier of Seville* (London), *The Musicians* (Berlin), *The Mulatto* (Dublin), and *The Fruit Seller* (Oslo), in which the artist, always with vigor, but sometimes with exuberance, sometimes with great restraint, explores a universe of simple forms in earth colors—a return, after centuries of religious art, to daily life. Then Velázquez went to the court of Spain.

Velázquez met Rubens on the latter's visit to Spain in 1638. From their encounters before the paintings of the Escorial, and their walks in the Castilian countryside, historians have drawn nicely balanced contrasts between the Fleming's aesthetic erudition and the Spaniard's naturalness. Certainly the two artists did not share the same tastes, but painters who paint peasants in all their rudeness are as aware of the art of the past as those who portray gods, heroes, and allegories.

In comparison to his other youthful works, this Spanish *almuerzo* (lunch) is so much more turbulent that we may well believe it is among the painter's very first compositions. The artist's intentions are various, and since he wished to express many things, he exaggerated the action, accentuated facial expressions, and even played a joke with the white collar and cap hanging on the wall to create the illusion of a face. Abundance is a sin of the young, but it is quite pardonable in this resonant work, joyous and as noisy as the banqueting musketeers of Haarlem painted by Frans Hals in the same period, and whose laughter Paul Claudel swore he could hear even before he walked into the museum hall.

BARTOLOMÉ ESTEBAN MURILLO (Spanish; 1616–1682)
Boy with a Dog
Undated
Oil on canvas, 30 1/2 × 24 1/4"
Catalogue No. 386.   Formerly Collection Duke de Choiseul

Because he painted a few tidy little boys with winning smiles who inspire in rich collectors a clear conscience about the happiness of living a life of honest poverty, of belonging to what is politely called "the little people," Murillo has become known as the "painter of little beggars." These images have been so popularized that they have blinded us to the rest of his works.

If we examine his work, we see immediately that this vein is far from being the richest in his career. Of the thirteen Murillos in the Hermitage, only one heralds the succession of little Savoyards with marmots and street urchins reproduced like pictures of movie stars. Not one of the Prado's thirty-nine Murillos is a maudlin child. The artist's works in Madrid show him for what he primarily was—a religious painter. A similar ratio emerges from the exhibition, *Treasures of Spanish Painting in France*, held in the Louvre in 1963—one beggar and four religious paintings. It was the same talent, the same brushes, that painted the *Angel's Kitchen*, the *Birth of the Virgin*, the *Immaculate Conception*, certain landscapes whose luminosity is already close to Boucher, and these figures done to draw a tender smile from the spectator.

One must therefore find the real Murillo, the man of mystical brightness, of eyes raised to heaven, of soft colors sometimes audaciously contrasted, before coming back to the street scenes whose descendants are so irritating. It is the same as with Greuze, where one must wipe away so many tears and discard so many pleading gestures in order to recognize the painter.

Here we are spared an anecdote of begging or delousing. The painting is in some way a portrait. Stripped of the suspicions invoked by all genre scenes, the work illustrates Murillo's joy in painting. Discreetly, and despite many prohibitions and weighty formulas, he handles his paint with pleasure, and fashions the boy's vest and short hair with delightful reticence.

NICOLAS POUSSIN (French; 1594–1665)
Landscape with Polyphemus

Painted in 1649
Oil on canvas, 59 × 78"
Formerly Collection of the Marquis de Conflans

There is nothing meager about Poussin's art. Each element attains its maximum richness and strength, whether a horse or a tree, a man or a group of men, a living creature or a corpse. Everything takes its place. We witness the triumph of a setting in which no accessory is overlooked, and every decorative element is used with the greatest ease. This is perhaps why a Poussin painting gives an impression of serenity and harmonious development.

It was in mythology that the painter sought the pleasure of existence. That antiquity had placed in this lost paradise (the history of humanity is a succession of lost paradises) frightful crimes and terrifying metamorphoses, that a pretty girl could turn into a tree or a handsome boy into a stream, that the division between man and beast was not yet entirely distinct, and that the laws of creation were still so fluid as to allow such monsters as the Cyclops—standing perhaps for some memory of the great mutations in the forms of terrestrial life—was a source of amusement for Poussin and in no way upset his sense of proportion. We see it in this picture, where country life flows calmly, like a slow stream over which birds are flying, between two singular levels of existence that belong to fable.

In the foreground it is perhaps the nymph Galatea who comes out of the water and twists her hair, while the satyrs watch. In Ovid, she says, "Sheltered by a rock, I reclined against the knees of my Acis, listening to the distant songs of Polyphemus."

On top of the mountain the Cyclops, sick with love, blows a flute made of a hundred reeds. The beauty of the painting lies in its calm, in the fact that the action is not yet engaged: the giant, seated on the summit, almost blends into the rocks and could easily pass unnoticed, while the foreground group might be a customary bathing scene of seventeenth-century painting. Between the two unfolds the life of the working peasants, the *fortunatos agricolas*. From the first, one feels the happiness of this land where untamed nature is favorable to man. Soon, no doubt, Polyphemus will crush Acis under a rock and Galatea will seek refuge in the water. Poussin has chosen a moment in which there is still no need to worry about the storm forming over the giant's head. In a little while, the peasants will return to their homes, the satyrs will vanish, and the Cyclops will turn around toward the happy valley. But not yet.

LOUIS LE NAIN (French; 1598–1648)
The Milkmaid's Family
Painted about 1640
Oil on canvas, 20 × 23 1/4"
Catalogue No. 1152

In the history of painting there have always been peasants. We see them working in the fields in the *Très Riches Heures du Duc de Berry*, dancing in Bruegel's canvases, in revolt in those of Dürer, who dedicates a monument to them. For Hugo van der Goes, they have been shepherds charmed by the birth of Christ; they have sold onions at market for Aertsen, caroused for Rubens, and decked themselves with ribbons to illustrate the joy of living for Fragonard. They have shown that, despite their rags, they were happy with a reed pipe and a glass of wine. They have been everything—the artisans of abundance, the pure in a society as lost as it is perfect, the living scandals of an unjust society, the representatives of an almost alien world, barely human, closer to the beasts. They have been so often used as illustrations of some system or other that they have rarely been themselves— that is to say, men.

Le Nain's peasants are as much models as are his nobles and bourgeois. The same faces reappear in one painting after another, and become familiar. The artist studied them in such depth that we are not surprised to recognize their descendants today on the streets of towns and villages. If our passers-by were to pose for their photographs, one imagines that they would present themselves no differently—the farmer would ask to be shown next to his tractor. The arrangement of a family group would be essentially the one used by Louis Le Nain in another Hermitage painting, *Visit to the Grandmother*, which is really a family portrait.

Le Nain was not, however, simply a popular local artist, isolated among the peasants of Laon. We know that the two elder brothers of this family of artists, Louis and Antoine, were invited to join the first Académie des Beaux-Arts, that engine of war destined to free the profession of the old structure of the Guild of Saint Luke. This means that they lived in Paris and were appreciated there. Consequently, the position of the Le Nain brothers in their time could only be that of artists who chose deliberately to paint scenes of their native region, in addition to executing large religious works for the churches. The same qualities are apparent in both categories—the lack of gesture, nothing in excess. The people are the same whether close to God or in their fields. There is little setting—a plain, the sky, a staff in the hand—and everything is simply but solidly assembled, forming a block. The most skillful painters of allegories and mythological scenes recognized the knowingness of this simplicity.

CLAUDE LORRAIN (French; 1600–1682)
Evening at the Port

Painted about 1649
Oil on canvas, 38 1/4 × 47 1/4″
Catalogue No. 1243.   Formerly Walpole Collection

In 1965, when 105 French paintings from the Leningrad and Moscow museums arrived in Bordeaux and eventually in Paris for exhibition, there ensued a scandal that swelled the circulation of the daily newspapers. A dealer had named fourteen works as suspect: two Lorrains, a Boucher, a mysterious landscape entitled *The Waterfall*, possibly by Watteau, two Courbets, the Clouet, the Boudin, a Le Nain, the Le Sueur, a Poussin, a Pater, a Hubert Robert, and a David. The affair grew rapidly, politics became involved, and the public was baffled.

In different circumstances, such as the publication of a scholarly study on the Russian collections, the affair would have been confined to a small inner circle of experts, but it was the exhibition in the Louvre that increased the public interest. Western Europeans are always rather suspicious of treasures kept so far away, like the Japanese when they speak of European collections of their own art. Legend would have it that both Russian and American collectors are easily cheated by forgers, and it is certainly true that forgeries have been purchased for Saint Petersburg as well as Texas. But Europeans forget how often they have been cheated themselves. Very few years go by without the "only" authentic version of the *Mona Lisa* being discovered in some European attic, the one in the Louvre being denounced as a fake. And moreover, the Russians had included some problematical paintings in the group.

A visitor to the exhibition might have questioned, as did Falconet in the eighteenth century, the other port scene by Claude Lorrain that was shown. That one, numbered 1782 in the Hermitage catalogue, was acquired from the Beaudoin Collection in 1784; a copy, seemingly superior in quality, is owned by the Queen of England. No questions, however, may be raised about the painting reproduced here, in which even the figures, according to the historian Charles Sterling, were, although it was not his habit, painted by the artist himself. Without doubt, a number of variants of this work are known, for Claude did not mind repeating himself. Moreover, people purchased his work in companion pieces: morning and evening, summer and winter, night and day. Purchasers thought less of the exceptional piece they saw before them than of the decorative possibilities of multiplying variants, to be scattered, repeated, and diluted on their walls. Landscape has never had the imposing presence of a human figure. And yet, no form of composition offers such an opportunity for reflection.

ANTOINE WATTEAU (French; 1684–1721)
Rest on the Flight into Egypt

Painted about 1717
Oil on canvas, 46 1/8 × 38 5/8"
Catalogue No. 1288. Formerly Gatchina Palace

"Watteau was successful in drawing small figures and grouping them well, but he was incapable of painting anything great," wrote Voltaire. We may wonder what the writer's conception of great painting was, but perhaps it would have been satisfied by this picture, an exception in the painter's *oeuvre*, and one of the rare paintings on a sacred theme that we have from his hand. Even for Voltaire, after all, the sacred was great. Experts see in this painting an interpretation of the Virgins of Van Dyck, Rubens, or Schedoni and point to a letter from Watteau to his friend Julienne telling how moved he was by the gift of a Rubens sketch from the Abbé de Noirterre. "Ever since I received it, I cannot rest and never tire of turning my eyes toward the desk where I have placed it as in a shrine." To thank Noirterre, the artist gave him a painting, probably the version *"alla Watteau"* of the Rubens that had been given him.

One painting does not make a chapter in a book, and almost nothing has been written on religious sentiment in the work of Watteau. We can only note that the rarity of such paintings in his career must have some meaning, and return to this "pastiche." It was undoubtedly born of a desire to analyze the work of another master. In this surprising composition, the group of four heads forms a central core about which everything is arranged—the base of the column, the movement of the clouds—probably not an original idea, but taken hastily from the model picture, for Watteau in this work was primarily interested in the intensity of light. One is tempted to compare his variations on the borrowed theme to Mozart's variations on Bach, the embellishment of strength with spirited invention. If themes or subjects may be said to belong to anybody, then the theme here belongs to another artist, but the seemingly odd arrangement, the rhythm of the painting, are certainly Watteau's. The slight swaying movement he gives his couples in raising them from the ground is easily recognizable. Who but he could have made of the Child a volume of such powerful tensions and nervous lines? Only Watteau's light brush could have created a sky in layers of quivering spume, rapidly, without insistence, simply to suggest the idea. There is also his way of delineating the face of the Virgin with a flow of light and five lines to indicate eyes, eyebrows, and mouth; the same idea may be found in a drawing in London's Municipal Museum. Watteau may have taken it from Van Dyck but, if he borrowed it, he used it in his own way, for this canvas is fully his. There is nothing more revealing than these deliberately ambiguous enterprises. Fragonard copied Rembrandt many times and sketched from Veronese, Rubens copied Titian, Ingres made drawings from Watteau. Each put himself into the other's character, but remained himself. Each took his bearings by the idea of the other, but none ever lost sight of his own truth.

JEAN-BAPTISTE-SIMÉON CHARDIN (French; 1699–1779)
The Attributes of the Arts

Painted in 1766
Oil on canvas, 44 1/8 × 55 1/4"
Catalogue No. 5627

Mariette did not really like Chardin, but he understood him well when he wrote: "On the whole, M. Chardin's talent is only a repetition of that of the Le Nain brothers." If it is obvious to us today that Chardin belongs to quite another aesthetic school than the Le Nains, it is nevertheless true that he continues their silence. It has been said that a certain stream of French painting, always discreet but not without strength in its reserve, runs through him (he is one of the painters whom Diderot described as mute because their works lend themselves poorly to literary comment) and continues up to Cézanne and Braque.

Of course, Chardin, painter of peaceful household scenes, only treated the subjects dear to the Dutch painters of the previous century, painting copper casseroles and dead game, washtubs and children's toys. This was not new, and the collectors of his time were entirely legitimate in comparing his works to the interiors of Pieter de Hooch or Ter Borch. But if the theme is the same, the spirit is very different. The picture is no longer an action or a presence seen within variations of light; it is an actual mosaic in which the pictorial surface, rich as it is, becomes like foam. Pastry and pottery—that is Chardin. The mosaic quality is concealed by placing the objects in perspective, and one takes such pleasure in the naturalness as to concede immediately that a vase as painted by Chardin is just like the vase itself. We sense the vibration of his work like the smell of fruit or freshly baked bread, and then pass on. But a Chardin, like a Vermeer, can be studied for hours, being full of surprises built on a complex and often well-concealed geometry.

The subject of the attributes of the arts (not to be taken any more seriously than the vanities, the five senses, preparations for a feast, and other pretexts for paintings) was fairly widespread in the eighteenth century. We find it in Subleyras (Toulouse), in Oudry (Schwerin), and in Vallayer-Coster (Louvre). It is not one of Chardin's most frequent themes, although he painted the *Attributes of the Arts and Sciences* in 1731 (Musée Cognacq-Jay, Paris), again about 1755 (Pushkin Museum, Moscow), and accepted a commission from the Marquis de Marigny for three over-door decorations for the royal chateau of Choisy: attributes of the arts, sciences, and music. Catherine II wanted him to do for Saint Petersburg what he had just done for the king of France and commissioned this painting for the Academy of Fine Arts. The artist exhibited a replica of the same size at the Paris Salon of 1769, where the catalogue described it as a "repetition, with some changes, of the painting done for the Empress of Russia." The copy is in the Minneapolis Institute of Arts and the changes are almost imperceptible. Both paintings show the same palette, the same right-angle ruler, the same architectural plan, the same statue of Mercury by Chardin's friend Pigalle, and the same rewards—money, a medal (perhaps the one the king of Sweden sent to Chardin in 1760), and the cross of an order either bestowed on him by the Swedish ambassador, Count Tessin, or (more probably, since the painting was to be sent to Russia) by Catherine.

JEAN-HONORÉ FRAGONARD (French; 1732–1806)
The Stolen Kiss

Painted about 1785–90

Oil on canvas, 18 1/8 × 21 5/8"

Catalogue No. 1300.   Formerly Collection of King Stanislas Augustus of Poland

It is often said that Fragonard's enthusiasm for painting slackened after 1789. His art would seem to be too attached to the joy of living to appeal to the new breed of men born of the French Revolution. Certainly the artist did not die at the height of his fame, but the austerity of the early Empire was foreign to his genius, and writers of his obituary were to characterize him rather disdainfully as a painter of fashionable scenes. But it should be noted that the slowing down of his production and the subsiding that one sees in the movement of his brush were not the result of successive changes in the political regime. As early as 1780, in his allegories of love, a chill came over his palette, and his nudes seemed suddenly to remember that they were supposed to be statues. And if Fragonard painted little between 1793 and 1800, it was because he was occupied in working with the commissions set up to reorganize the museums and in teaching art. He became, in fact, one of the most active reformers of the arts in the young Republic, and it was perhaps for this reason that the Empire neglected him.

Fragonard painted few interior scenes. He loved sky and trees, haystacks and clouds, and misty light that murmurs like tall poplars. If he had to go indoors, it was into an alcove, or a farmhouse where he was amused by the animals that sometimes thrust their heads through the window to look at the humans. And if he resigned himself to locking the door, it had to be when the covers were being pulled back on the bed.

The Stolen Kiss, often linked with *The Lock* and *The Contract*, lost paintings known only through engravings, belongs to the artist's last period and shows some kinship with works composed at the end of his life in collaboration with Marguerite Gérard. Some critics claim that the disciple dragged the master down to the level of primness and affectation. Such is hardly true of this painting, in which the treatment of fabrics, of precious woods, of the wool in the rug, and the soft flesh of face and throat becomes a delight going beyond the anecdote of a love trembling for fear of discovery. The painting has often been compared to Dutch scenes of the preceding century, no doubt in order to contrast the lively spirit of the long diagonal in modulations of gray that runs across the picture with the static elements, however well treated, in such an artist as Ter Borch.

JEAN-AUGUSTE-DOMINIQUE INGRES (French; 1780–1867)
Portrait of Count Guriev

Painted in 1821
Oil on canvas, 42 1/8 × 33 7/8"
Catalogue No. 5678.   Formerly Narishkin Collection

Ingres went to Italy in 1806. When, in 1815, all his French patrons of the kingdoms of Rome and Naples returned to France, he thought his career was finished. But he found that he was able to support himself and stayed on in Italy until 1824. The artist's fame was primarily national and this is the only Ingres in the Hermitage. In Moscow there is a Madonna that he painted in Rome.

Painted in Florence in 1821, this portrait shows Count Guriev, the Russian ambassador, in the discreet finery of a man of fashion, imperious and very knowing in the ways of the world. A century earlier, another Russian ambassador had had himself painted in Spain by Carreño de Miranda. His portrait in the Prado shows him in a superbly embroidered Oriental costume with a dagger in his belt. The two paintings illustrate the evolution of the Russian elite in one century. In the seventeenth century, the Russians were still odd foreigners; by the eighteenth, they were perfectly integrated into the Western world.

From a distance, this portrait presents a harmony of blacks and blues crossed by a flash of red; it is strong and much more daring than the portrait of Granet, painted fourteen years earlier in Rome, in which the figure is also placed before a panorama. The landscape is here limited to suggestions— the mountains and a few umbrella pines above the white houses indicate Italy. More important is the storm in the sky behind the sitter, by which the artist has perhaps tried best to characterize him, and not without a Romanticism akin to Chateaubriand's *René: "Levez-vous vite, orages désirés . . .* (Arise quickly, ye wished-for storms)."

Closer examination shows a very subtle modulation in this reduced range of colors, with extremely fine, intense notes in the mauve variations of the cape lining, the sheen of the gloves, and the sharp lines of cuffs and collar. The white of the linen takes on a cutting metallic quality that seems to strengthen the sitter and make him even more remote. Ingres said, "A painting is always beautiful when it is true. Our errors do not always come from not having enough taste or imagination; they come from not having been natural enough." The painter almost contradicts himself with one amusing detail. He could not quite decide whether to represent entirely the top hat on the left. He judged it sufficient to suggest its presence.

EUGÈNE DELACROIX (French; 1798–1863)
Arab Saddling His Horse

Painted in 1855
Oil on canvas, 22 × 18 1/2"
Catalogue No. 3852.   *Formerly Kushelev-Bezborodko Collection*

Like so many poets and painters of his time, Delacroix had always dreamed of the Orient. Then suddenly, when he was thirty-five, he joined the staff of the Count de Mornay, whom Louis-Philippe had appointed as Ambassador to the Sultan of Morocco. The painter remained in Morocco for four months, staying principally in Tangier, and making a long cross-country trip with the count to reach the sultan's residence in Meknès. A great deal has been said of his fascination with the antique influences remaining in Moroccan costumes and customs. He wrote, "The Greeks and Romans are here at my door. I am highly amused at David's Greeks." But if Morocco took the place of Italy in his letters, when he abandoned his pen for his box of watercolors, he filled countless sketchbooks with drawings and notes, setting down with exceptional precision the realities of Moroccan life—the shapes of turbans, varieties of weapons, decorations on pottery, manner of playing the drum. He discovered what was false in the Parisian idea of the fabulous Orient, and learned that the sun burns out colors, so that to be exact he had to use gray in such a painting as the *Entry of the Crusaders into Constantinople.*

Delacroix used his Moroccan and Algerian notes (and he spent only a few days in Algeria) all his life. The chronology of his career shows that he sent "African" paintings to the Salons of 1834, 1838, 1841, 1847, 1849, and 1850 and that, even in the year of his death, he painted an Arab mountain battle, using a setting such as those he had sketched near Meknès. Morocco was thus a permanent source for his painting.

He learned something more during his trip. "I only began to do something passable with my voyage to Africa," he wrote, "when I had forgotten enough petty details so as to recall in my paintings only what was striking and poetic. Until then, I had been pursued by that love of exactitude that most people take for truth."

This painting illustrates that remark perfectly. There is nothing of an ethnologist's report. This is simply the encounter of a man and an animal, the contrast of light garment and dark hide treated in small nervous strokes that crackle with light, while the large red saddle becomes the bright center of accord between rider and steed.

CAMILLE PISSARRO (French; 1830–1903)
La Place du Théâtre Français, Paris

Painted in 1898
Oil on canvas, 25 7/8 × 32"
Catalogue No. 6509. Formerly Shchukin Collection

To avoid the attentions of bystanders while painting from life in the heart of Paris, the Impressionists had a habit of working from the windows of their studios or of their friends' apartments. Monet did so, as did Manet, but nobody was so fond of this kind of upper-story vision as was Pissarro, who systematically moved from hotel to hotel seeking rooms with views of the city. In this way, he painted the Boulevard Montmartre, the Carrousel, the Tuileries, and here, the Place du Théâtre Français. The Impressionist city views were a form of the art of urban landscapes that flourished abundantly in seventeenth-century Holland, eighteenth-century Venice, and nineteenth-century Rome, with the difference that in a Canaletto, for example, one finds the image of the Doges' Palace or the Church of the Salute, the most famous city monuments, while the Impressionists were more interested in the light and color of Paris itself. It is true that palaces and churches worthy of attention were no longer being built—architecture had become chiefly an urbanism of comfortable homes.

It is perhaps significant that although these painters were sensitive to old quarters of the city, and liked the suburbs, the countryside, and the facades of Norman churches, they also looked intensely at the milling crowds and long facades of the newer neighborhoods. They loved the modern Paris of their own time, and besides, it was where they lived. Their exhibitions were held in rented premises that were often poorly arranged for the presentation of paintings. The Neo-Impressionists even rented the reception rooms of the Hôtel Brébant on the Boulevard Poissonnière. This was in 1893, when Pissarro had already left the young group of artists to whom for some years he had lent the prestige of his fame.

From his windows, Pissarro watched the light change on trees, buildings, and sidewalks. The aging painter leaned over the balcony on the Boulevard Montmartre from morning to night, watching the life on the street below, the lighting of the street lamps, the passing carriages, the small silhouettes of pedestrians coming and going. Thus he painted a series of documents, as luminous as they are sociological, that commemorate the life of a city street.

He moved to the Hôtel du Louvre for this painting. *La Place du Théâtre Français* offers a lovely vision of springtime in Paris in mid-afternoon. The chestnut trees open fresh new leaves above the square where several tram lines converge. This is Paris as seen by the pigeons and roof-tilers. The famous theater shows only its pale facade and false columns. In order to set off the trams, and the lines of passengers waiting to board them, Pissarro reduced the size of the people and carriages further away, which makes the square seem larger than it really is. The fluidity of the work comes from the light that flows over the ground, and it is this gaiety, more than the faithful portrayal of the subject, that holds our attention.

136

EDGAR DEGAS (French; 1834–1917)
Woman at Her Toilet

Drawn in 1885
Pastel on cardboard, 20 1/2 × 20 1/8"
Now in the Pushkin Museum, Moscow

This pastel is very similar to a group that Degas sent to the last Impressionist Exhibition in 1886, and which was described in the catalogue as a "Series of female nudes, bathing, washing, drying themselves, combing their hair or having it combed." Public reaction was lively. Huysmans declared that the pastels had something of a "cripple's stump," and other critics denounced the artist for his misogyny. It is true that Degas had always shown some sadistic traits, noticeable as early as 1865 in his *Misfortunes of the City of Orléans*, full of captive, maltreated women. However, this tendency took a less cruel form in his studies of dancers and nudes. The new tensions revealed in these figures were far removed from the positions of tortured women. Degas may have spoken sharply about the female animal, but it is not possible to believe that he devoted his life to painting women just to revenge himself. The Moscow pastels are among the most favorable of his studies, this one in particular.

We notice at once the pearly flesh, its harmonious juxtaposition to the blue of the dressing gown draped behind it, and the delicacy of a nape reminiscent of the grace of Watteau's drawings. Most striking, however, is the strength with which this sensual sweetness is placed within the square of the paper. One of the last works of the aged painter is the profile of a dancer. Degas went over and over the drawing. The line of the waist and the lifted arm became so thick that it exists by and for itself at the expense of the volume. In the Moscow pastel, the color is admirably delicate and harmonious, but the strength of the work lies in its clear lines, the curves of the leg, the hollow at the waist, the thrust of the buttocks. The finest line in this pastel is the spinal furrow, and it is for this that Degas composed the work. He drew other pastels to show a long tress of hair crossing the entire surface plane, or the appearance of the back in the foreground when a dancer bends over to fasten her slipper.

Here there is nothing of the "cripple's stump." This is simply the daily rite of every woman at her toilet in the cramped space of tubs and basins. Degas watched for other charms of this rite even on the tram, which he often took, according to Paul Valéry, for no other reason than to see some woman in front of him, unmindful of her surroundings, adjusting the veil of her hat or touching up her coiffure.

PAUL CÉZANNE (French; 1839–1906)
Woman in Blue

Painted about 1900–1904
Oil on canvas, 32 1/2 × 28 1/4"
Catalogue No. 8890.   Formerly Shchukin Collection

A woman puts on a blue silk dress, open over a blue yoke. She dons a delightful hat whose flowers soften with a feminine touch what would otherwise be a rather military look. She takes her pose before the painter. Whatever century he may belong to, when he faces his model, he is either so profoundly moved that his subject influences his pictorial expression, or he remains indifferent, so accustomed to the woman that she can no longer surprise him, or not curious enough to evoke her reality. Or he may simply wish to let nothing distract him from his experiment of the moment, whether it be to try a new color, to attempt a more rigorous construction of volume in space, or even to tangle some arabesques in the four corners of the canvas. When the work is completed, the woman will still be part of it, and not necessarily as a minus quantity. Sometimes indifference serves her image as well as passion.

The model may have been the artist's wife, Mme Hortense Cézanne, *née* Fiquet. The painting conveys both her presence and her reserve—that is to say, a kind of habitual withdrawal. It is from this figure of a woman that a whole new lineage of modern human representations descends. We must never forget that the continuity of Cézanne's experiments was assured only *in extremis* by the advent of the Cubists, more than forty years his juniors. When his first exhibition opened at Vollard's in 1895, the painters who surrounded him, from Émile Bernard to Maurice Denis, Camoin, and Roussel, undoubtedly esteemed him, but they took no account in their own works of what was new (and very old) in his paintings. "I am too old now," said Cézanne, "I remain the primitive on the path that I discovered."

Only after his death were there painters to set out on this path, but such is the law of inheritance. Those who followed him too closely could not reach his level and limited themselves to an imitation of technique or even of subject matter. Those who were stimulated by his contribution rapidly discarded what they had taken from him, as if the influence of a master lay only in appearances. Appearances aside, Cézanne, who was never very comfortable with his contemporaries, the Impressionists, found that by this transfiguration, as total as it was unapparent, he had renewed the reality that one finds in Poussin, as in Le Nain, Delacroix, and Chardin. In a work as sullen and powerful as this portrait, he demonstrates the need for balance and severity, the need to go beyond the happy accidents that have not ceased to be the rule in French painting.

The portrait has been damaged and bears several long, conspicuous scratches.

PAUL CÉZANNE (French; 1839–1906)
Road near Mont Sainte-Victoire

Painted in 1898–1902

Oil on canvas, 30 3/4×39"

Catalogue No. 8991.   Formerly Morosov Collection

The eleven Cézannes in the Hermitage and the fourteen in the Pushkin Museum cover the period from before the Franco-Prussian War of 1870 until the artist's last years. There is a little of everything: the Île de France and Provence, portraits, still lifes, a sketch for the famous *Bathers*, and even that strange Mardi Gras scene that foreshadows the Pierrots and Harlequins that many Cubists would turn to when, tired of breaking up form, they thought they could stay in the Cézanne tradition by using his subjects. The whole range of Cézanne's complex genius is represented in Russia— all of it—sometimes unconsciously, sometimes deliberately, pointing in the same direction.

One cannot travel in Provence and pass the Mont Sainte-Victoire without thinking of Cézanne and marveling at the great number of versions that he left of its image. This is no doubt due to the fact that he regarded this huge, naked rock, rising amidst the plains and valleys, less as a mountain than as a subject. Around 1885, he saw it as one of those peaks that Poussin or Claude Lorrain placed in their compositions. There was even an aqueduct in the plain, and the long, slender succession of arches enticed him like a reminder of Rome. But by 1900, Cézanne no longer painted the Classical landscape so easily evoked by the setting of Provence. The pines, the cottages, the roads, the corrugations of the terrain, the line dividing the blue sky from the blue rock—all have lost the customary reserve imposed on reality by narrative or description to yield to the intensity of their own physical presence. The physical painting itself is no longer concealed, and moves into the foreground. This landscape would seem to illustrate a sentence of Monsieur Teste in which Valéry attributes to this pure thinker the concerns of a painter: "I wish to borrow from the (visible) world only its forces— not its forms, but what makes its forms. No narrative. No background. Simply the feeling of matter itself—rock, air, water, vegetable matter, and their basic properties."

After Cézanne, this desire to arrive at primal truths produced many paintings that supposedly expressed them, yet finally disclosed nothing but threadbare abstractions. Abstraction is never alive unless it is indivisible, a private key for everyone—that is to say the world—this darkness open to our constantly renewed light.

ALFRED SISLEY (French; 1839–1899)
Village on the Banks of the Seine

Painted in 1872
Oil on canvas, 23 1/4 × 33 1/2"
Catalogue No. 9005.   Formerly Shchukin Collection

Three paintings in Leningrad and three in Moscow show that Shchukin and Morosov were well aware of Sisley, a painter who does not impose on us a vision of the world, but offers himself as a sensitive spectator. Scholars are always a little embarrassed by Sisley. They appreciate the quality of his work, but are unable to draw from it the profoundly new elements that they find in equivalent paintings by Renoir or Monet. The fact is that Sisley lends himself badly to theory and is easy to grasp emotionally. He is rather in the position of the Dutchman Hobbema, who is placed second to the innovator Ruisdael—no one knows what to make of the marvels of his landscapes.

There are hundreds of paintings like this *Village on the Banks of the Seine,* showing a river with well-placed trees in the foreground such as artists have always drawn. Photographers take picture postcards from the same angle. A certain taste for "views" remains constant throughout the centuries. Can an artist assert himself without renewing the formula?

When Monet later looked at a few rocks emerging from the sea, or when Van Gogh painted a clump of laurels, the perspective had clearly changed. But this is no reason to deny the sensitivity of Sisley's more common approach. Thanks to the quality of his painting, Sisley reaches inside the most modest formula to make us feel his presence and veracity. To seize, to apprehend, to grasp—all this can happen at many levels.

Impressionism in this painting has not yet reached its maximum intensity. It is still partial to shadow, to the accents of light that ripple over the river bank. But however cautious it may be, it reveals a man who, without daring the extremes, could see the tranquil charm of a village on the water and convey his pleasure in looking at it.

Here there is nothing, or almost nothing. But to those who know how to look, there is all the depth in the world.

CLAUDE MONET (French; 1840–1926)
Haystack

Painted in 1886
Oil on canvas, 24 × 31 7/8"
Catalogue No. 6563.   Formerly Shchukin Collection

A haystack, a field overrun with poppies, rows of trees spaced evenly in the countryside form this modest Monet landscape, more modest than the *Rocks of Belle-Île*, and composed in the studio, as was done before it was possible to carry tubes of color directly to the scene. From now on the artist plants his easel before any landscape that suddenly strikes his fancy. Working from nature depends on both artist and subject—there are unfavorable seasons and unsuitable regions. Hence Monet's journeys across France, from one town or village to another. Poissy, for example, had seemed attractive in passing, but did not inspire him when he settled there, and he soon had to leave for Dieppe. There is something of the hunter in a landscapist—he cannot function without game.

Fields of poppies always fascinated Monet, but at this period he did not dare look at them for themselves as he looked at the sea. He wanted the red strip and placed it on his canvas, quivering and bent by the wind in the greenery. But he did not let himself go as he would some years later with the gold of a wheat field, assured of the fine animation of the picture by the forms of the haystacks. Thus the haystack in this painting is the prelude to a prodigious process of liberation. Kandinsky was aware of this and wrote, "I found myself standing before a painting that represented a haystack, or so the catalogue said, but I did not recognize it." This reflection on reality led to the adventure of abstract art.

Monet, who considered himself an eye open on the world, who only painted with his subject before him, thus traced a passage that the Abstract Expressionists would begin again, thirty years after the *Water Lilies*. Basically contradictory ideas may give birth to comparable works, a fact that should cause some reflection on the futility of theories. In 1910, while Monet was still alive, Kandinsky in *The Spiritual in Art* recommended caution. "If from today forward, we sever our ties with nature and cut ourselves off from her entirely without any hesitation or any looking back, if we are content only to combine pure color with freely invented form, the works we create will be ornamental and geometric, not very different at first sight from a necktie or a rug."

Monet may have sensed this danger. He never wished to undertake anything except in the uncertainty of the pursuit of landscape, assured of a natural risk in which the painter, skillful as he is, takes his chances in a necessarily uncertain struggle. He knows that there is the equal possibility of triumph or failure, and how enriching this is. One should always have an adversary. It is the best way to renew oneself, to grasp a way of being.

AUGUSTE RENOIR (French; 1841–1919)
Woman in Black

Undated
Oil on canvas, 24 3/4 × 20 7/8″
Catalogue No. 6506.   Formerly Shchukin Collection

"Black," said the painter, "is the queen of colors." This is perhaps surprising from an Impressionist since the term "Impressionism" evokes a sensation of light and the luminosity of color. But Renoir, more than Monet, was sensitive to the lesson of the museums. He always thought that he needed something else besides an eye keen enough to follow all the subtle vibrations of light on people and objects. He never forgot Frans Hals's manner of rumpling a cuff, or how Velázquez knotted a scarf and Watteau made satin rustle. For these masters, black had not been merely a background, something to make other colors stand out; it had been a color in itself.

The *Woman in Black* is one of a series of portraits painted in about 1873 when Renoir moved to the Rue Saint-Georges. At that time, he told his friends that he felt he had "arrived," not at a remunerative stage of his career, but at a point where he felt strong enough to control all the influences he had accepted and to achieve the ease in figure painting that Impressionism had afforded him in landscapes. For Renoir, to have "arrived" meant to be more natural.

The period was a difficult one. The first Impressionist exhibition in 1874 had been greeted with laughter. The painters, however, were aware that they were a force to contend with and that there were encouraging voices in the press and, thus, among the public. For Renoir himself, the public existence of the movement had brought a commission from Hartmann, the music publisher, for a portrait of his wife (Louvre). The auction sale, in 1875, of works by Renoir, Monet, Sisley, and Berthe Morisot at the Hôtel Drouot, a daring idea, was almost a disaster but did enlarge their audience. Chocquet wanted a portrait of his wife, and soon commissions for portraits of Mme Henriot, of Jeanne Samary, and of Mme Charpentier, the wife of Zola's publisher, showed that Renoir was advancing socially and being accepted by people of taste. Renoir's striking female portraits have lost none of their charm. How often it happens that an old woman dies, and the newspapers describe her as a young girl who had posed for Renoir! We can say of a woman that she was a real little Boucher or a stunning Renoir, but never that she was a Cézanne—which only shows the harmony that existed between Renoir and his models.

The portrait of Mme Hartmann is rather surprising. The lady appears in her upholstered setting wearing an elaborate dress that is in the style of the period and at the same time suggests a court costume of the seventeenth century. Renoir well knew that the bourgeoisie of his time hankered after royalty. The female figure in his *Loge* of 1874 (Courtauld Institute) is much closer to present-day feeling, and the face of Mme Alphonse Daudet (1876, Louvre) seems almost contemporary. Yet no portrait is closer in spirit to our own time than this anonymous *Woman in Black* whom Renoir painted with as much freedom as he ever permitted himself toward the models on whom he lavished his genius.

VINCENT VAN GOGH (Dutch; 1853–1890)
Bushes

Painted in 1888

Oil on canvas, 28 3/4 × 36 5/8"

Catalogue No. 6511.   Formerly Shchukin Collection

A clump of white-flowering laurel, a few irises—this is Provence. Vincent van Gogh arrived in Arles in February, 1888, after two years in Paris. His life moved swiftly in Provence and when he painted this picture, probably in August, he had less than two years to live. A little unsettled by his loneliness, he had already considered asking Gauguin, whom he had known in Paris, to join him. But Gauguin's brief stay in Arles was to be a psychological and aesthetic crisis, temporarily interrupting the flow of what was in the process of being born in such a work as this.

From the first moment of his arrival in Provence at the end of winter, Van Gogh was astonished by the brilliant color and the movement of plant forms. He drew and painted many orchards, fertile plains, flowering almond trees, beds of sunflowers, and as the sun became brighter with each passing month and extinguished the colors, he followed the changes of tones within the patches of light. This painting constitutes one of the most advanced stages in this experiment. Form has become less and less visible; what the artist has really painted here is the impact of sunlight on leaves and flowers that in their transparency let the blue of the sky pass through them. Van Gogh, it has been said, renounced Impressionism here, but this is not very obvious. He retained the process while introducing more of himself than he had yet dared. This bush becomes literally a burning bush, which is not astonishing in the work of a man who always wished to express more than nature's simple charm. Here we have the germ of the giant cypresses that, in 1890, will rise like flames into a sky of spinning suns.

VINCENT VAN GOGH (Dutch; 1853–1890)

Promenade at Arles (Recollections of the Garden at Etten)

Painted in 1888

Oil on canvas, 29 × 36 1/2"

Catalogue No. 9116.   Formerly Shchukin Collection

When Gauguin arrived in Arles in 1888, he was full of ideas that tormented Vincent van Gogh. Referring perhaps to such works as *Bushes*, but more probably thinking of the Divisionist landscapes done in Paris, Gauguin said, "Vincent is still floundering around in Neo-Impressionism." Gauguin decided to set his friend on the path leading to significant painting, done not from life but in the studio and in a silence conducive to total expression—away, for example, from such distractions as laurel leaves quivering in the sun.

Van Gogh, who awaited this orientation from the depths of himself, as a renewal of all the experiments of his first paintings, as proof of the somewhat hampering effect that Impressionism must have had on him, then wrote, "Gauguin gives me the courage to imagine things." But that what the Dutchman imagined in Provence should be a memory, a recollection of his family's garden at the parsonage at Etten, would seem to indicate that his comrade's influence had been unconsciously rejected from the start.

The aesthetic collaboration of the two men produced two parallel works on a related theme. Gauguin painted two women of Arles in the hospital garden (Art Institute of Chicago). A sloping wall, bearing a vague resemblance to a faun's head, and a gate take up the foreground. The women, almost completely hidden under their shawls, pass between clipped hedges; two sailors in the background watch them. The sailors' sarcastic comments are easily imagined, and Gauguin himself invites us to do so by entitling the picture *Les Vieilles Filles* (The Old Maids). It is a satirical painting, a criticism of manners. It is the same size as Van Gogh's picture, which has nothing satirical about it. An old woman in a red-flecked shawl and a younger one holding a red parasol (whose long hand might have been painted by Picasso in his Blue Period) walk among undulating cypress trees through a flowered setting in which a peasant woman, bent over like Millet's figures, is working. The canvas exudes melancholy.

Here Van Gogh has found a way back to the work of his youth. By following Gauguin's advice, he has discarded Impressionism and cultivated the arabesque. He apparently believed at the time that he had changed, but he later wrote, "I bungled that thing I did with the garden at Etten." Once Gauguin left Arles, Van Gogh returned to his true path, which was not so much to imagine as to re-create, to conquer by his will the landscapes he chose.

Great emphasis has always been laid on Gauguin's influence on Van Gogh during their tragic stay in Arles. Let us not forget that there are Gauguins of this period (such as the *Café at Arles*, Pushkin Museum, Moscow) which show that the influence was reciprocal.

PAUL GAUGUIN (French; 1848–1903)
Tahitian Pastoral

Painted in 1893

Oil on canvas, 33 7/8 × 44 1/2"

Catalogue No. 9119.   Formerly Morosov Collection

As Gauguin wrote to his friend Daniel de Monfried in December, 1892: "I have just finished three paintings, two of equal size and a larger one. I think they are my best, and since it will be January first in a few days, I have dated the best one 1893. Oddly enough, I have given it a title in French, *Pastorales tahitiennes*, since I cannot find a corresponding title in Kanak. I do not know why, but by using pure Veronese green and vermilion *ditto*, it seems to me like an old Dutch painting or an old tapestry. Why should that be? Besides, all my paintings look insipid in color."

The painter's comments show great self-confidence, a conviction that his work was valuable, and, at the same time, uncertainty. This self-doubt may have been one of Gauguin's reasons for returning to France in that very year, 1893. He had spent more than two years in Tahiti from June, 1891, to July, 1893. His first sojourn in Oceania was only temporary. The second, begun in 1895, was to be final.

Gauguin's question is the more surprising coming at this moment, when the French title on his canvas shows that he had remained closer than he believed to the world he had wished to leave behind. Heightening his colors was evidently not enough to make the difference. Painters in Paris were doing the same thing and Gauguin was well aware of it.

He had, in a certain sense, gone to Tahiti to find what Poussin had imagined: man attuned to nature. Poussin had located this agreeable concord in the lost paradise of mythology. Gauguin found it in native villages where women went about bare-breasted, where horsemen rode bare-back, where the fruits from the trees belonged to those who picked them, where life was still simple and the social system so elementary that the law could be wise and kind. Much has been said about the artist's blossoming as a result of his contact with a primitive world that still seemed free. It is necessary to note that he painted nude Breton Eves on the dunes near the seashore, and that he had seen small peasant boys bathing nude in the river at Pont-Aven. Thus, he had already sought Classical themes, and it is easy to infer that when he painted these Tahitian pastorals he wished to go beyond visual satisfaction. He knew that exoticism would not guarantee the value or originality of his work, and simultaneously discovered the futility of themes and systems.

There was nothing more to change in art; the artist had to be himself and accept himself, however Classical he might seem. In this spirit, five years later, Gauguin was to paint his great masterpiece, *Where Do We Come From? What Are We? Where Are We Going?*, a work that falls within the tradition stretching from Mantegna to Courbet. The highly civilized artist had assimilated the savageness of the remotest part of the world.

PAUL SIGNAC (French; 1863–1935)
Marseilles
Painted about 1907
Oil on canvas, 18 1/8 × 21 5/8"
Catalogue No. 6524.   Formerly Morosov Collection

The last Impressionist exhibition in Paris, in 1886—at which Degas showed his nude pastels—also included Gauguin, Odilon Redon, and Pissarro. It was the latter who had invited two newcomers: Seurat, who exhibited *A Sunday Afternoon on the Island of La Grande Jatte*, and Signac with his *Apprêteuse et garnisseuse* ("Two Milliners"). Impressionism offered no resistance to what Félix Fénéon was quick to christen Neo-Impressionism.

It was a curious movement, which did not correspond to a particular generation of painters, Seurat having won over artists older than himself (Cross, Angrand, Dubois-Pillet, Luce, even Pissarro, old enough to be his father), and having found in Signac, four years his junior, the disciple who was not only the theoretician of the movement but the only one besides Luce who would maintain its aesthetic throughout the normal length of an artist's career.

Signac, moreover, finds himself singularly isolated in the chronological scale of art history. He was born the year Delacroix died. His closest seniors were Van Gogh, older by ten years, and Gauguin, older by fifteen. Like Lautrec, neither of them was more than temporarily responsive to the Divisionist experiment. Signac's most immediate juniors were Bonnard, Vuillard, and Matisse, respectively four, five, and six years younger than himself, and they did not go along with his research very long either. The publication (in 1899) of his book *D'Eugène Delacroix au néo-impressionnisme* and Seurat's first exhibition in 1900 led to the conversion around 1904 of such artists as Matisse, Marquet, Camoin, Manguin, Vlaminck, and Van Dongen, who later turned rapidly toward Fauvism, the opposite of Divisionism. Signac held out, and was even the only one, after Seurat, to attract international attention.

This marine landscape showing a sailing vessel in the port of Marseilles dates from about 1907. Fond of pleasure boating, Signac always liked harbors, from Saint-Tropez to La Rochelle, from Venice to Constantinople. He belonged to the generation that saw the disappearance of the great three-masted schooners. The one in this painting is already guided by a steamer.

The painting shows once again how much marine artists have contributed to the history of painting. Distinct from the landbound, such artists as the Van de Veldes, Turner, Jongkind, Boudin, and Signac have created a continuity of works from the remotest elements, first of all sea and sky, in other words from that formlessness of which Valéry speaks in relation to Degas—a formlessness to which the first luminists imparted structure.

HENRI ROUSSEAU (French; 1844–1910)
Promenade in the Luxembourg Gardens

Painted in 1909
Oil on canvas, 15 × 18 1/2"
Catalogue No. 7716.   Formerly Shchukin Collection

Rousseau painted the music kiosk in the Parc Montsouris, the paths of the Parc de Saint-Cloud, the hills of Clamart where the Parisians go to pick lilies of the valley, the entire suburban area of Sunday promenades, with the diligence with which he invented his most mysterious Mexican forests. Probably he no more drew his Parisian subjects from life, or planted his easel in front of the Eiffel Tower, than he made sketches of Central American monkeys. We know that in his studio he made his pupils paint from picture postcards, and the master undoubtedly worked in the same way. Some day the photograph of the monument to Chopin may turn up. It is not easy to find the Dubois statue in the Luxembourg Gardens today. The woman who rents chairs swears that "the Germans destroyed it during the war." One must insist, and finally the pedestal is found half-hidden in the bushes. The female figure, raising a shoulder from the stone to disclose a face ravaged by tuberculosis, no longer stares at a bronze bust of the composer. The commission charged with the collection of nonferrous metals during the war did not fail to collect Chopin, and today nobody is much interested in restoring a sculpture by Dubois. Rousseau's Paris has vanished. His Paris was not the city of historical masterpieces; it was the Paris of his own time, now out of fashion and which no one cares to preserve. The curve of the garden path, the lawns still neatly edged by the same little hoops, remain the same, but the old-fashioned charm of the Luxembourg Gardens had begun to fade even before Rousseau painted this corner.

This landscape was painted in 1909, Rousseau's year of glory, in which he exhibited his portrait of Apollinaire, accompanied by Marie Laurencin as his muse, at the Salon des Indépendants. Vollard bought some of his paintings; he associated with Picasso and Delaunay. The critic Uhde was respectful, and Ardengo Soffici wrote the first lengthy study of his work. It may have seemed to Rousseau that the sarcasm and persecution that had surrounded him were to be avenged. It was the year before his death.

We may note that the artist did not find in the popular quarter of Plaisance (now in the process of being leveled by the bulldozers), where he lived and whose spirit he expressed so well, a favorable reception from his equals, the small shopkeepers and pensioners. He was only accepted by the avant-garde artists of his time, those whose painting was the most remote from his own idea of the beautiful. Only they were capable of recognizing that there was in Rousseau a great artist, and also the greatest of all so-called naive painters. The species is far from extinct, but no one has yet equaled the Douanier.

HENRI MATISSE (French; 1869–1954)

Harmony in Red (Red Room)

Painted in 1908

Oil on canvas, 70 7/8 × 86 5/8″

Catalogue No. 9660.   Formerly Shchukin Collection

That Matisse should only have begun painting in his twenties does not seem to have deprived him of the energy that youth usually squanders on experiments that are as haphazard as they are profitable, and at the same time seems rapidly to have given him an adult vision of art. In this he differs from Picasso, who began his flawless career as a child prodigy. Matisse took up painting after the normal age. He had delicate health, but the kind of delicate health that does not prevent a man from living to the age of eighty-five. Obviously he quickly overcame his delayed beginning, since by the age of thirty, which is when artists generally discover themselves, he had entered on his true path. Soon surrounded by young artists, he passed with them through the temptations of Neo-Impressionism, and then, regaining a grip on himself two years before painting this *Harmony in Red*, outdistanced the others with such stunning rapidity that few younger men were able to catch up with him for many years to come.

A few Russian collectors, Shchukin first of all, and some Americans, like Gertrude and Leo Stein, realized what was happening in Matisse's studio and bought paintings that thus vanished from the exhibitions. As a result, the best work created by the artist in his forties remained, until recent years when traveling exhibitions and book reproductions put them back into circulation, less well known than the seductive odalisques from around 1925 and the collages of his final years—the latter renewing these earlier experiments with audacious rigor, seeming to be a sudden novelty when they were really a return to the source.

Some hints, however, of his development had been given at the time. The first state of this painting, called *Harmony in Blue*, was exhibited at the Salon d'Automne in 1908. Shchukin wanted to carry it off to Moscow, but Matisse asked for postponement and sent instead the *Harmony in Red*, an exact replica of the composition in another color. The pattern that the artist used in 1906 in his *Joy of Life* (Barnes Foundation) is recognizable, but his arabesques here are no longer a return to Poussin's harmonious balance. Matisse had left behind the museums and his own Arcadia to be himself. Much of the future is to be seen in this red, and the themes borrowed from the patterns of eighteenth-century painted toile de Jouy perhaps foreshadow the collages of woven elements of which artists were to avail themselves so often in later years.

HENRI MATISSE (French; 1869–1954)

The Dance

Painted in 1910

Oil on canvas, 102 1/2 × 154"

Catalogue No. 9673. Formerly Shchukin Collection

There are thirty-five Matisses in the Hermitage and sixteen in the Pushkin Museum. With one exception, dated 1940 and a gift of the artist's devoted secretary, Mme Delektorskaya, all were purchased by Shchukin and Morosov before 1914. No other country offers such an ample view of the artist's experiments between 1896 and the First World War.

After *Harmony in Red*, which was to be placed in his dining room, Shchukin commissioned three large panels for the successive staircase landings in his Moscow palace, once the home of the Troubetskoy family. The artist, thinking of the spectator climbing the stairs, had the idea of depicting for the first landing the rhythm of the dance, for the second the restful effect of music, and for the third the repose of reclining figures in their essence. The higher one climbed, the closer one was to come to peace. But there were some difficulties. When Shchukin saw *The Dance* and *Music* at the Salon d'Automne in 1910, he felt uneasy about having such conspicuous nudes in his home. But he was carried away by the strength of the works, and the two paintings (for only two were executed) were finally hung in Moscow. In 1940, Matisse went to see them and did not protest the red overpainting that masked the genitals of his musicians.

The twin paintings mark a high point in Matisse's career. Did the painter perhaps discover that at this level the air, and possibly art as well, became rarified? He did not return to the theme for many years. But in the circular movement of the dance and in the musical group where the musicians seem posed like chords, he had formulated not something new, but something long forgotten. As the Cubists had found shortly before, and as the abstract painters were soon to discover, Matisse had perceived that it was necessary to return to purity of line and color, to sweep away the excesses and uncertainties with which painting was encumbered and start afresh.

These ideas were already present in *Harmony in Red* and the *Game of Bowls* (1900), also in the Hermitage, but had not reached complete fulfillment. There the color was already applied in a hasty wash, but the line did not always avoid the pleasure of the arabesque. In the staircase paintings, Matisse rejected all the temptations of color and line. In these enchanting and ascetic paintings he does not allow himself anything that he has loved. We might say that Matisse adopted Monsieur Teste's maxim, "One must enter into himself armed to the teeth."

ALBERT MARQUET (French; 1875–1947)
Harbor of Naples

Painted in 1909
Oil on canvas, 24 1/2 × 31 1/2"
Catalogue No. 9150.   Formerly Morosov Collection

In his review of the Salon des Indépendants of 1910, Guillaume Apollinaire speaks of Marquet's entries, hanging not far from the paintings of Matisse, Friesz, Manguin, Puy, and Vlaminck. "As simple as they are," he wrote, "Marquet's two canvases are impressive. The painter looks kindly at nature, with a little of the sweetness of Saint Francis. Both his scenes, the *Sea at Naples* and *Dutch Street with Flags*, reflect this kindness, this tranquillity, this joy." The *Sea at Naples* may be the painting now at the Hermitage. We may keep Apollinaire's terms of kindness, tranquillity, and joy, and forget the comparison to Saint Francis which dripped from his pen. Some terms apply more to humanity than to painting, and there is not much literary content in Marquet's landscapes; they are, purely and simply, paintings.

Marquet was one of the Fauves and availed himself of pure colors. Does one then stop being a Fauve by no longer using vermilion? But to go on painting the bright flutter of flags in the clear air when one arrives in the South, where the light is so strong that it obliterates color, would not that be to betray one's principles, one's duty to be the most intense? The artist must now master a whole range of blues to express the light of Naples. This may explain Apollinaire's renunciation of his technical vocabulary in the face of this painting and his adoption of a phrase with which one characterizes a man. He admired the fidelity of the colorist.

For this painting is intense and a perfect pictorial exercise. At the top is the blue of the sky, a pristine blue that scarcely vibrates. Then comes the white to form clouds and the curve of Vesuvius. A darker line marks the horizon and the blue breaks up into quick brushstrokes, mingling here and there with a few patches of umber. The artist thus does the whole panorama in three colors, blue, white, and umber, and life is imparted by their vibrations. What is strange is that this austere technique harmonizes perfectly with a smiling sentiment of nature. It is this gentle and sometimes amused expression that one retains from Marquet's work—which does not mean that it hides the rigor of the artist.

The Hermitage owns nine Marquets and the Pushkin Museum eight.

PABLO PICASSO (Spanish; 1881–1973)

The Encounter

Painted in 1902

Oil on wood, 59 7/8 × 39 3/8"

Catalogue No. 9071. Formerly Shchukin Collection

It was Matisse who introduced Picasso's work to his patron Shchukin. From 1908 until the declaration of war in 1914 the Russian was a constant visitor to Picasso's studio, where he purchased fifty paintings, being the only collector to follow Picasso in all his early experiments. He drew back, it is said, only before *Les Demoiselles d'Avignon*, but this did not prevent him from purchasing works that were no less harsh, such as the *Dryad* and the *Farmer's Wife*. Shchukin, unlike Vollard, who found it impossible to be Picasso's dealer in this Cubist phase, reacted with sensitivity to the new idea, while Morosov, converted in his turn, did not hesitate to buy the Cubist portrait of the hesitant merchant.

The Encounter, possibly inspired by silhouettes perceived at the women's prison of Saint-Lazare in Paris, was painted in Barcelona when the artist returned to Spain after his second stay in Montmartre. It is one of the early Blue Period works, in which Picasso discovered that the limitation of color brings with it particular obligations of drawing. The work was not unique for its period. We find the same sobriety in Isidro Nonell, a Catalan artist whose figures are as overwhelmed by misery, closed in on themselves, confined in blocks of suffering; also, no doubt, in Puvis de Chavannes. An equally striking resemblance is shown by Gauguin's figures: for example, in the great canvas *Where Do We Come From? What Are We? Where Are We Going?* Picasso may not have seen all the references that art historians make in discussing his works, but there is no question that he was always very sensitive to the ideas of his time and that, from the start of his career until his death, he always lived in the present in such a way as not to be separated from his contemporaries. This communing with others never meant submission, but a taking of what he needed for his personal development. In these two upright figures, the modern framework also recalls the structure of Romanesque and Gothic sculpture while remaining a highly personal painting that has to be reckoned with from the start. Here we find Picasso and no one else.

The drawing of the face on the right has a severity that foreshadows the pre-Cubist figures of 1906. Picasso here purifies the eminently realistic theme of poverty with a clarity not always demonstrated in some of his more deliberately emotional figures. He combines this abstraction of despair with a simplification of style that borders on nobility. Let us not forget that when he painted this picture he was twenty-one years old.

PABLO PICASSO (Spanish; 1881–1973)
Portrait of Vollard

Painted in 1910
Oil on canvas, 36 1/4 × 25 1/2"
Formerly Morosov Collection

Legend has it that Vollard slept as much as possible and that during his siestas the prices of his paintings never stopped rising. Picasso made his own contribution to this legend by showing the dealer with lowered eyelids, which may suggest that he is enjoying one of those famous naps. Actually Vollard is reading. During the same period, 1909–10, Picasso also painted portraits of Wilhelm Uhde and of Daniel-Henry Kahnweiler, the dealer who took over his Cubist works from the hesitant Vollard. Kahnweiler's eyelids are lowered too, an uncharacteristic expression for him. If the painter extinguished the gaze of his models (and he continued to have many and to sustain in Cubism the traditional theme of the portrait), it was doubtless less out of respect for their personalities than because it would have been difficult for him to open two eyes in the crystallized mountain that he called a portrait.

Of course, the general rhythm, the arrangements of light and volume are those that can be recognized in every portrait from Frans Hals to Renoir. The mass that is Vollard is set off from the background by a series of tiny luminous splinters forming shoulders, temples, and skull—the man is there. Yet at the same time he disappears, for his body is criss-crossed with staircases, tunnels, sections of walls, piers, and corridors. Since reality is identifiable only by its proportions—the entrance to a cave or the gaping cuff of a sleeve have the same shape—the deliberate uncertainty here adds to the difficulty of recognition. The Vollardian nostril resembles an arch, barely emphasized by slightly more light than falls on the entire theatrical arrangement which seems to hollow out the stomach and is nothing but the transcription of the letter that he holds in his hand. Is this a game of appearances? Not at all—it is the painter's method of distributing the rhythm that he extracts from the four corners of his canvas.

It is some sixty years since the invention of such portraits, and their appearance remains as fascinating as ever. The problems of portraiture have not ceased to interest modern painters, who attempt many experiments with a steadfastness that may seem surprising—especially when we remember that photographers have largely replaced painters in this area of human representation. If we are still intrigued by such images, this must be less for their novelty (which wears out quickly) than for the way in which they shatter the surface of tradition to give us, after all, only an amplification of Cézanne's methods of constructing form—that is to say, exposing the ancient formula of the portrait to its final modification. This is the beginning of the end of a tradition. We might add that Picasso did another portrait of Vollard in 1915, a very precise drawing and as true to life as this portrait is transfigured.

DATE DUE	
NOV 17 1995	
JUN 11 2003	
GAYLORD	PRINTED IN U.S.A.